BEYOND *Traditional* TRAINING

ken marshall

BEYOND *Traditional* TRAINING

develop
your skills
to maximize
training
impact

First published 1999
Reprinted 2001

Kogan Page Limited
120 Pentonville Road
London
N1 9JN
UK

Stylus Publishing Inc.
22883 Quicksilver Drive
Sterling
VA 20166–2012
USA

British Library Cataloguing in Publication Data

A CIP record for this book is available from the British Library.

ISBN 0 7494 3028 1

Typeset by JS Typesetting, Wellingborough, Northamptonshire
Printed and bound by Clays Ltd, St Ives plc

DEDICATION

To Beamish, whose love, encouragement and devotion inspire me to achieve my dreams and ambitions.

CONTENTS

AN INTRODUCTION TO YOUR THREE-DAY PROGRAMME

'The worst days of those who enjoy what they do are better than the best days of those who don't.'

I will begin at the end. This, as all SMART trainers know, is the best place to start. I will be your personal coach and will give you one-to-one tuition in becoming the best you have ever been.

Welcome to your three-day Master Class Beyond Traditional Training Programme. The pages between these book covers contain the wisdom, knowledge and practical know-how of my popular training programme, all condensed in an easy to read and implement format, crammed with all the gems, examples and fun of the live programme. I believe it will change forever your view of training and how best to train people, including yourself, in the art of higher performance.

My aim is to take you on a great journey of discovery. And like all journeys that you prepare for effectively you need to be very clear of your destination. This book will be the means to achieve an important end: to become a better trainer than you are currently. And I say this to you, no matter how good you rate yourself today, no matter how good others rate you today. I want people to say this about you: 'Hey, that trainer was good when I attended the course two years ago, but boy, you should see how good the trainer is now.'

This book is aimed at both trainers and personnel professionals employed full-time by organizations, and independent training and management consultants of all disciplines. This is not a book on better presentation skills, nor is it a book just on training tips and tricks of the trade (although you will find plenty of those along the way). It has been specifically developed in order to assist the professional who has to deliver training sessions, workshops, courses or complete programmes.

It is designed to upgrade your current thinking habits and methods as well as your current training habits and methods. It is also designed to be a constant reference manual for the serious developer of self and others.

If followed and acted upon, the actions listed within these pages will move you up to the next level of training performance. And then when you are ready, it will help you move up to the next level again.

It will place you in a position to operate beyond traditional training practices. With this book you can achieve your best training ever. And be in a position to repeat that feat year after year.

Always remember this: as important as your client or boss is, the person who has the real power over your career in the training and development profession is the delegate. Without consistent highly favourable reviews you will lose valuable repeat business or promotion prospects. Your professional reputation, which you hold so dear and worked so hard to achieve, can only be further enhanced by following the key principles and strategies contained within this book.

My end then, besides ensuring you have a learner-friendly coach and teaching process, is to raise your game. I have a very clear picture of the end result and that is you being significantly better than you are today as a direct result of reading this book and putting its key strategies into practice. You will not have to complete the whole book before you start to enjoy its many treats and reap its many benefits. You will be able to pick up and run with many of the techniques and strategies that I will share and teach you after just one or two brief readings of chapters or sections. Always carry this book with you as part of your essential reference material.

I believe this will apply no matter how many times you pick this book up, dip in, and re-read these pages over the years. This book should always be close at hand because I believe that it will be your route to super training achievement. Please believe me, because I am totally serious about this claim. I can help you, through these pages, become a much sought-after training professional. This book really is your ticket to lifelong high-income work in the training world.

Let me take you through a brief overview of what this book contains and how I intend to increase your training impact. Together we will go through the Beyond Traditional Training experience, together we will explore the lows and the highs, the dos and the don'ts, the wows and the woahs, the applause and the boos.

You will quickly learn how to power your way to the top of the SMART training league. I promise to help you become the very best at what you love to do – helping others to improve. (And if you don't love helping others improve, then I can tell you here and now, you're in the wrong job.)

Together we will make a quantum leap of personal achievement. I say *we* because I know that by writing this book for your benefit I will reap a fantastic reward from the experience too. Now stay close and listen well as you read.

A BRIEF OVERVIEW

Consider the book you have in your hands to be a complete set of practical workshops, for I have put onto paper what I cover in my three-day SMART TRAINER workshop.

I will take you through an intensive three-day Beyond Traditional Training programme. You will find your book is set out in three distinct parts; each day of your programme will take you through four high impact sessions. These have been designed to give you real hands-on techniques that you can put into practice immediately.

Keep it close at hand for the tips and tricks of the trade, quick response activities, and dealing with difficult delegates and awful training venues (and boy, have I seen a few of those).

Use it to evaluate your own progress and personal development into the realms of the high-earning training professional. *Beyond Traditional Training* will take you to a new level of training professionalism. You will discover just what it means to be a SMART TRAINER (where would we trainers be without our mnemonics) in the truest sense. Implement the steps laid down in the SMART TRAINER process and WOW them every time.

THE AGENDA

This is how your personal SMART TRAINER guide shapes up:

Skilful – in the art of developing self and others.
Mastery – of all SMART training skills and attitudes.
Adroit – to deal with difficulty and take challenges in your stride.
Ready – to act at a moment's notice if required.
Transfer – of skills, knowledge and excitement from you to your students.

Trustworthy – to maintain and keep training-room confidences.
Resolved – to make every learning experience fun and worthwhile.
Authority – on your chosen subjects.
Inventive – in order to create new experiences with old topics.
Navigator – of the learning journey to take your students on an adventure.
Energetic – to keep the pace and fun at the appropriate levels.
Rewarding – so that everybody wins with a SMART TRAINER.

This allows you to examine exactly what is expected of a SMART trainer in the Beyond Traditional Training sense. I think you'll agree that all of the above is quite correct and noble. Maybe you could think of different words to use, but let's not get side-tracked by semantics. Let's keep focused on the outcome: high impact training that moves us toward a more effective approach to training others. You always want to give your students a learning experience that not only works but also is fun and motivational into the bargain.

You also want to ensure that your students are so impressed with your training that they return to work fired up, and able to put into immediate practice the very techniques that the client has paid you to train their people in. What a bonus! Not only a fun experience but a serious and rewarding outcome too.

We all want the same things at the end of the day – a job we really enjoy and continue to get a buzz from, happy students and delighted clients. (Don't be put off by the word 'client' by the way. Even if you are employed as a trainer you still have clients to satisfy. They're called line managers, directors and the boss!)

WHAT'S IN A NAME?

I have called this book *Beyond Traditional Training* because that is where I want to take you. Why? Because 'traditional', while it may have its merits in many areas of life, is boring in training. Your audience may tolerate traditional training but they won't be inspired by it. They won't be motivated by it. And by definition they most probably won't learn from it, or if they do, then the chances are high that they won't act on it.

To explode a myth (the first of many, rest assured) may help to throw some initial light on this. Many people believe that knowledge is power, knowledge is strength. They are wrong. Knowledge is just knowledge. The real power and strength lie in the use of knowledge.

And that is the trainer's real job. To transfer knowledge, the accompanying 'how to' skills and techniques all wrapped up in inspiration, get-up-and-go and let-me-at-it. Put yourself in the delegate's place every time. As a delegate I don't just want to be taught – I want to be moved to do something different that will make my life a damn sight easier. Now train it like that.

I also want to help rid the training profession of below average and arrogant trainers who do nothing more than belittle delegates through their own superiority complexes. They do this while undermining the training profession as a whole and make life harder for all genuine trainers who operate with integrity and real concern and professionalism for their trainees' welfare and future success.

I know from experience that you can only truly enter the realm of Beyond Traditional Training when you master the skills of viewing all of your training inputs and activities through the eyes and emotions of your delegates.

So let us begin our journey to the place of true professionals. To the place where tradition receives its just respect but remains where it really belongs, in the past. For Beyond Traditional Training is where we've all got to be heading, all of the time and that is into the future.

ACKNOWLEDGEMENTS

I would like to make the following acknowledgements as a show of appreciation for the support and co-operation I was given in successfully completing this project.

Peter Thomson of the British Business Consultants & Trainers Academy for the use and adaptation of the PEQ™ (Personal Effectiveness Quotient) and for forming the academy for the likes of all of us lonely independent trainers.

Tom Lambert for his ideas, suggestions and encouragement for attempting such a huge project like this while still carrying out the business of training.

Jane Stewart, my first boss at my first training department, who took me under her wing, helped me discover mine and then taught me how to fly.

PART ONE

LAYING YOUR FOUNDATIONS ON SOLID GROUND

'Regardless of the distance to be travelled, every journey begins with the first step.'

(Jim Rohn)

YOUR FIRST IMPORTANT STEP

This is your first step of an incredible journey. It is incredible because it is about you and your professional life. Make sure you have fun, but remember its seriousness. I can promise you this: act on the fundamental principles of SMART training contained within the pages of this book and you will improve. You will succeed and you will gain on many levels of your life.

In this part you will discover and learn how to consistently achieve your best year ever in training. The four chapters contained within this part will take you on a journey where you will collect the knowledge, techniques and the all-important know-how to create the first draft of your Personal Development Plan.

These four chapters are the equivalent to the first day of my Master Class workshop – Beyond Traditional Training. Each chapter is like receiving key information and strategies that you can action, through a series of high impact training sessions. The chapters/sessions within this section are:

1. Self-perception versus reality;
2. Upgrading your mental software for success;
3. The critical questions essential for becoming a SMART trainer;
4. Preparing the foundations of your plan of action – Action Plan Part I.

Please feel free to highlight key areas of text and write pencil notes in the margins for future reference and assistance. You will also find self-discovery inventories to complete and score. Learn the truth about your current style of training. You will also be taken through, step-by-step, a series of critical questions that will enable you to develop your own abilities and strengths, easier and faster than ever before.

You will also discover that all of the elements of this three-day Master Class workshop can be adapted and used on your own courses and programmes. This will become one of the books that you will always pack when you prepare for any training event. A word of caution – don't lend it to another trainer; the chances are high that you won't ever see it again!

HOW TO READ THIS BOOK

This may seem an unnecessary piece of information but research shows that most people do not know how to read a book to the best advantage.

We are all busy people and finding the time to fit some extracurricular reading into our already overloaded schedules may seem nigh on impossible. So here are some pointers that may well help you in your important quest for continual self-improvement.

- First, scan down the contents; this will give you the big picture. You will see that the book, just like the Master Class workshop that it emulates, progresses logically and builds on strong foundations.
- Secondly, flick forward to any section or chapter that particularly catches your eye; scan this to satisfy your curiosity.
- Thirdly, make a decision as to how working your way through this programme would be best achieved for you and your personal circumstances.

Just like the SMART trainer that you will become from following these lessons, break the task into manageable chunks. I have found that by disciplining myself to read a minimum number of pages every day I can forecast just how long it will take me to get through and how many books I can complete in a year.

In my own case, as an example I aim to read a minimum of six pages per day. Now, I prefer to read just before bedtime[1] and completing an average of just six pages will see me finishing the book within one month, about five working weeks actually. Whichever time of day you prefer is really down to personal choice and preference; the key here is to just make sure you *do it.*

In this country people read an average of less than one book on self-development/non-fiction per year. You don't need to be an Einstein to realize that if you can average around 12 per year you're going to be at a distinct advantage when it comes to achievement and success.

I encourage you to write in this book. There are dedicated areas for you to do so, but I also want you to feel free to write in the margins and highlight key pieces of text. This book was written with the intention of it being a working document. It will be the equivalent of attending one of my three-day Master Class SMART trainer workshops, which would cost you over £1,000. I know that if you, like me, are a bit of a bibliophile, then writing in books does not come easy. After all, to us book nuts marking a book's clean pages is tantamount to vandalism, but in this instance it is OK because this is officially a workbook, guidebook and reference manual and therefore permission to write on the pages is granted.

Once you have familiarized yourself with your programme's content, work your way through each part completing the self-discovery inventories, activities and action plan drafts as you go. Just like my workshops, the methods of learning will be:

- my input;
- your input;
- self-discovery exercises;
- activities;
- action plans.

The style of your programme is:

- informal;
- relaxed;
- non-judgemental;
- open minded;
- constructive and instructive;
- fun!!!

Enjoy the book as you enjoy the experience that will improve your job satisfaction, your earnings and your professional reputation. Your journey to Beyond Traditional Training begins here with me as your personal coach.

At the back of this book you will find details of how to contact me if you need to. Please feel free to write, phone or e-mail me if you have any questions, need clarification or have any other feedback; you will be most welcome. I promise to do everything I can to assist you in your quest for total success.

Read, enjoy and act. You deserve the success you are about to achieve.

Note

1. This is the best time of the day to take in new information.

1

SELF-PERCEPTION VERSUS REALITY

'Effective communication is 20 per cent of what you know and 80 per cent of how you feel about what you know.'

(Jim Rohn)

Your learning objectives in this chapter

By the end of this chapter you will have learnt how your:

- self-delusion can be a real danger to your personal development and success;
- self-delusion can hinder your delegates' learning of new skills;
- attitude to feedback can prevent you from achieving the status you deserve;
- ability to make personal decisions can shoot your training career into orbit.

How do you come across to your training course delegates? How do they see you? How do they hear you? How do they feel when you are talking to them? How are they judging you as you take them through their learning experience?

Questions, questions, questions. And all aimed at that highly emotive subject, your personal performance. What you need are answers if you are to rapidly progress to the dizzy heights of Beyond Traditional Training methods. The SMART trainer does not shirk from honest appraisal, even if it is a little bit painful at times. Hey! None of us is perfect. I think now is a good time to explode another myth. 'Practice makes perfect.' Well, practice is essential to the learning, developing and improving process, but it won't make you perfect, for we are mere mortals and incapable of perfection in its truest sense. Practice moves us forward in progress and improvement through increased confidence, which in turn helps us improve, which in turn builds our confidence, which in turn helps us improve. And so the cycle gathers momentum.

Through this chapter I will switch your perspective and teach you how to apply objective and de-emotionalized feedback to your own performance as a trainer. This is an essential skill for the SMART trainer who wants to achieve Beyond Traditional Training status.

It is because we have been brought up to believe that we can and should be perfect that we get angry with ourselves if we feel we are falling short of this heady ideal. We chastise ourselves many times a week for not being able to do something as well as we feel we should. It is usually something quite small or insignificant in the wider scheme of things. This often forces us, out of habit, to become very inward focused. Initially this makes us feel more mental anguish. With our minds operating on inward focus mode we develop a process called 'self-deception' and only see what we know will make us feel good.

We all know people who work at being managers, directors, doctors, trainers, or whatever, who really believe that they are great at what they do, but everyone else experiences something very different.

THE DANGER OF SELF-DELUSION

Many years ago, in another life, I was a training officer, training milkmen in customer care and sales. I remember a guy who had been on the same milk round for over 15 years. He didn't want to be on the training course, as he believed that he knew all there was to know about customer care and selling. About a month after the training course I did some follow-up and visited a few sites to see how my delegates were doing with their new-found skills and strategies that I had taught them.

I spent a few hours with my 'you can't teach me anything' friend. I travelled with him while he made his deliveries and introduced me to 'his' customers. He seemed to genuinely believe that every single one of his customers loved him, almost to the point of worshipping the ground he walked on. I had no reason to doubt him.

Back at the sales depot I spent some time talking with a few of the relief milkmen, the guys that cover when the regular milkman goes on holiday. One of the relief supervisors asked how I had got on with 'Mr Know it all'. He then shared with me his experiences with the customers every time he covered for our friend. He told me the customers' true feelings for him.

'I didn't do a survey or anything,' he began, 'but people would ask me, as they furtively glanced up and down the road and over to where the milk float was parked, where their usual milkman was. I told them he was on holiday for a fortnight and that I would be looking after them for a while. "Thank goodness for that," they'd say, "he is always so arrogant and rude".'

As a rough estimate, about 6 out of 10 customers didn't have a kind word for him and the others never mentioned him. A classic example of self-perception versus reality I think. It was an area that I was set to explore in much more depth and detail.

OBJECTIVE FEEDBACK IS CRUCIAL

Our milkman generated strong emotions in his customers; unfortunately they were negative ones. Yet he believed they were positive emotions. Technically he was doing the right things. However, his communication style was way off beam, and he didn't know it or at least wouldn't admit to it.

To admit to his shortcomings and negative traits our milkman would have had to admit he was well short of perfect. That would be uncomfortable. When anybody attempted feedback to this person it was received as criticism. That would have been uncomfortable. He would have rejected this and placed the blame squarely at their feet. That would be easier to live with and less effort.

I have known trainers who, on reading the 'happy sheets' (more on these later), have dismissed negative feedback as being the fault of the trainees because they obviously missed the point. This is something that I have done in the past. I now look at it very differently. I use a technique that I learnt many years ago to de-emotionalize the situation because, as I discovered, emotions have a lot to answer for.

Emotions are powerful and are the cause of all the world's problems. They're also responsible for all the world's greatest moments. So let us find a balance that we can work with more effectively.

In order to take on board the information we receive as feedback in a constructive and useful way, we need to learn to make it neutral. That is easier said than done. We all love to be told how good we are and what a great difference we make. As Maslow discovered, recognition is one of the most powerful forms of motivation. And as Dr Eric Berne discovered when he was researching transactional analysis, the natural child ego state within all of us seeks recognition.

The problem is our emotions. They get in the way of clarity and realism. This is of course because we are emotional beings. So, how do emotional beings stop being emotional long enough to see the real picture and not the picture that they prefer?

First, let's establish just what is reality. Is reality what you see and feel, or is it what other people see and feel as they interact with you? I know the general school of thought is that perception is reality and because everyone has their own perspective of looking at things then that is, in essence, true.

However, if we take this from the standpoint of trainer and delegate then the bias leans more heavily toward the delegate's perspective. Why? Because you are stage centre and have the biggest impact in terms of communicating outward. You are there to serve the purpose of the training events outcome, against which you are being consistently measured as you progress through your training sessions with your delegates.

Delegates will be measuring you consciously and sub-consciously all through the training event, in varying degrees. They will be measuring your performance on a number of levels simultaneously – how you look, how you sound, the words you use, the body language displayed. Have they discovered early enough in the course what's in it for them so that they know their reason for being there? They will have a logical mental checklist that they will tick off, either consciously or sub-consciously, that will lead them to an emotion that tells them whether you're someone they want to spend their time with or not.

Your window of opportunity to put over a positive image is small. And I am amazed at just how few trainers utilize this time effectively. Some even ignore it all together, believing it to be an ineffective use of time. Oh, how wrong they are! We will explore this in detail in Part Two where I will share with you real-life case studies of how to guarantee poor feedback.

To know is to grow

It is imperative that we open our eyes and the rest of our senses to take in important information being fed back to us. We are receiving this feedback all of the time. We must train ourselves to become increasingly sensitive to it.

Now, by sensitive I don't mean we allow ourselves to get upset. Initially though, while you're still adjusting to receiving everything about you, warts and all, you will feel a little down about it now and again. Don't worry about this, as it's quite normal.

So, don't be put off. When I started out as a trainer, many years ago, I used to allow myself to become quite hurt by criticism, until a few key points became clear to me. The vast majority of people don't know how to give feedback constructively. How could they? No one is ever trained to do this. Certainly schools never trained us in the skills of constructive criticism. In fact from my experience both as a pupil and father of two who had a keen interest in his daughters' education, most teachers were some of the worst offenders – but then no one taught them either.

When most people partake in telling others how they are messing up, they do just that – tell them that they are messing up. They then usually add in some exaggerated personal defects as a means of justifying saying that they messed up. And they very rarely, if ever, tell us how we could improve.

All in all, they tell us what we don't want to hear, couched in terms that offend, communicated in a manner and tone that are offensive. They offer no alternatives, while claiming they're our friend and want to help us. Yeah, so why do I now think you're an offensive, insensitive, ignorant buffoon talking out of the back of your neck? No wonder we shy away from feedback.

There is a way round this dilemma. Just because these untrained critics that we are surrounded by and expose ourselves to personalize their feedback, it doesn't mean we have to take it personally.

Making allowances

You must learn to make allowances. Allow for the fact that:

- they are untrained in this specialist skill;
- they can only phrase their feedback in the way they know how, which is based in emotional terms;

- they are copying those who have given them untrained criticism in the past;
- they may not know what the hell they're talking about;
- they might be spiteful and riddled with envy at your success.

When receiving the feedback that you must go out of your way to get, in order to progress to the realms of Beyond Traditional Training, first assess the situation and circumstances surrounding it. Then you can take each piece of critiqued information about your performance and honestly explore whether or not it really does fit you. This becomes easier the more you practise it. Tell yourself to ignore any personal details and emotional observations. Concentrate only on concrete examples of actual behaviour, such as the method used to communicate your message, like activity, session input, video, etc.

I have found this process to be very helpful when taking feedback from course delegates, whether directly or via evaluation sheets. Evaluation sheets, or as I have already labelled them, 'happy sheets', have a process all of their own as you will discover shortly.

Becoming a feedback junkie

Strive to receive feedback on your training performance from as many sources as you can and as regularly as you can. I don't mean become obsessive about it. Regular should mean every few months, say three or four, and make a full assessment of the information you are receiving. Look for trends in the feedback data, where two or three delegates each course or workshop have remarked about a certain session not working that well, or that a certain video left them feeling cold or neutral.

Evaluation sheets are just one source. While they can be useful, if the questions are SMART questions and not dumb ones, they are often limiting and tend to be biased towards the feel good, or feel bad factor generated during the course.

There are two main problems with evaluation sheets. The first is the way they are structured; the second is end-of-course euphoria. Some sheets have tick-box scoring (some methods are better than others) with a few questions to encourage feedback with a little more detail. However, the quality of the feedback is in direct correlation to the quality of the questions. Most evaluation sheets that I have come across either ask pathetically composed closed questions so as to limit everything to basic 'yes', 'no', 'don't know' answers, or are left blank. Others have such wide-ranging open questions that demand such deep thinking that they also limit everything to basic 'yes', 'no', 'don't know' answers or are left blank.

While we need good quality feedback from our delivered courses, SMART trainers know that their delegates, after two days of challenging, fun-filled learning are feeling a little battle weary and mentally fatigued. They don't need the krypton factor or trite, glaringly worthless questions. The worst I have come across was when training for a company that insisted that the delegates ended the course by filling in a four-page evaluation document consisting of 30 questions. The form stated that it would only take them five minutes to complete! My point here is, why ask all those questions if you don't want them answered properly?

This brings me to the second problem area. I have found, with a few exceptions, that no matter how brilliantly the course has been delivered and how enthusiastically the delegates have received their training, when the end of the course arrives they are ecstatically happy that they can go home to their loved ones, a rest and a long cold drink. Hence the term 'happy sheets'. It is for this reason that I prefer very little reliance on tick-box scoring and more emphasis on SMART open questions. Questions that are very tightly focused on how you performed in delivering the key learning messages are the only ones that really count. For example: 'Which two items of the training course did you find least useful? And why?'

I will take your through some detailed evaluation sheets in Part Three, where you can design your own tightly focused feedback tools. These will direct you toward reality and away from self-delusion. You want to know how it is. How it *really* is – the good, the bad and the indifferent. Then you are in possession of really constructive information that you can use to fine-tune your hard work towards perfection. You know it makes sense, but there is a down side. When you read the bad bits it's a little painful. Until, that is, you change your perspective. You will explore how best to do that in the next chapter when I share with you key strategies on 'upgrading your mental software'. First though, let's have a look at the other sources of feedback available for the SMART trainer to take full advantage of for improvement.

OTHER SOURCES OF FEEDBACK

I have used a feedback activity built into the workshop. This was run as the last session of each training day and allowed the delegates to work alone as a group. The trainer sets the session going and then leaves the room for 20 minutes.

The group elects a scribe and then they work their way through a set of evaluation questions, noting key points on the flipchart as they progress. Everybody gets to air their views, likes and dislikes, what worked well, what didn't, what they learnt, what they discovered and what skills and knowledge they had confirmed.

On returning to the main room, the trainer then sits through a group presentation of the day's events from the viewpoint of the group. You might think that this process would most likely create a bias against being overly critical and that, maybe, with the trainer present, the group would be less outspoken about the elements of the workshop that worked less well. This doesn't tend to happen as there is safety in numbers, and individual delegates feel brave enough to talk about their true feelings about something.

Feeling exposed

This process can seem quite scary and appear to expose the trainer unnecessarily to a barrage of largely destructive and unfair criticism. This, I can assure you, will not happen. Safety in numbers works both ways. It generates its own governing rules and forces the group to channel their feedback objectively. You would assist this process by ensuring the evaluation questions were SMART questions[1] and moved the session on in a constructive way. Those in the group who have a tendency to allow their own prejudices and emotions to get the better of them are tempered by the more fair-minded and focused.

In my experience, more often than not the harshest criticisms are about course administration, the quality of the coffee and venue conditions. As most of my training takes place within the clients' own organization and on their premises, these are all things out of my control. I always make sure that the client sees the group feedback flipchart sheets though, but only as long as there is no way of identifying comments from individual delegates.[2]

The camera never lies

As much as most people absolutely hate seeing themselves lumbering across a television screen, warts and all, video footage of your performances is great feedback.

I strongly recommend that you do this every once in a while. The hassle of setting up the camera, seeing the little red light blinking away at you as you perform is well worth it.

When you get to play back and view your camera work you need to take into account a few factors. The first viewing should be just that, a viewing. At this stage do not try to critique yourself. Just watch it, listen to what you said and get used to seeing yourself on the small screen.

Mentally prepare yourself first and then watch the video again. Your preparation will be along the lines of raising your awareness of what to look out for. Things such as speed and clarity of speech; when you know something very well yourself and you have been delivering it many times over a prolonged period, you can easily allow your explanation of the topic to become blurred. Check voice volume, especially if outside sounds invade the training room. Are you automatically adjusting your volume up as you should be? Do you have any quaint mannerisms, excessive verbal repetitions, poor body language, visual image problems[3] or plain bad habits that need attention?

In this area the camera really doesn't lie. You do, however, need to know the difference between the professional image you need to portray and the credibility-destroying image so many trainers (both employed and independent consultants) take into the market place every day.

View your video a few times, noting down any key points that you feel would enhance your performance if worked on. Don't get disheartened or unduly worried. Always look at these sessions as a great way to develop yourself, to work on your own strengths and to dilute your weaknesses.

You only need to video the odd session. I would recommend filming yourself delivering the opening session of the day. On a two-day workshop you could also film a session towards the end of the second day. Between 20 and 40 minutes for each session would be ample for you to get a good taste of what your delegates are receiving from you. Repeat this process at least once a year.

I have come across many trainers who are the world's worst when it comes to practising what they preach. They sell their clients and their delegates the virtues of continuous development, of how critical it is in an ever-changing world, and then pay scant regard to their own. Well, not if you want to join the SMART trainer set and be counted among those who achieve Beyond Traditional Training status.

Colleagues

Another form of receiving regular feedback on how you are coming across to your delegates is to call on the help of a trusted colleague – a fellow professional whose opinions and objectivity you know and trust.

Decide what you want your feedback partner to focus on. Try and get them to give you the personal experience of what an attending delegate would think and feel about the session.

REALITY VERSUS SELF-PERCEPTION

As professional trainers we know that the only way people can change for the better is by being allowed to look at themselves as others see them. From this they discover which elements need to be played up, which factors need playing down, which ones need to be eliminated, and what gaps exist that need to be filled and bridged with new skills, strategies, techniques and knowledge.

Remember, knowledge isn't strength or power, but the use of our knowledge most definitely is.

I see my job as a Peak Performance Specialist as being the person who, in the first instance, calms the fears of the nervous learner. For learning means mistakes and a journey out of the warmth of the comfort zone, into uncharted territory. I then take a large mirror and hold it up so that the learners in my charge can see themselves as others see them. Through this process I allow them to discover for themselves just how they come across, how they sound, how they behave to the people they long to influence the most.

Once they have seen what they are doing well, usually by default, they can put it into practice by design. They can also use the new skills and strategies I will train them in to replace the negative traits and destructive behaviours that have dogged their professional and personal lives for so long.

This process works well for all trainers that use it, but it can always be improved upon. So, as professional trainers, as SMART trainers, it is good practice to turn the mirror on ourselves every once in a while, to ensure we practise what we preach and teach to others.

AN ATTITUDE THING

At the core of this behaviour, which is inherent in all top performing and high earning training professionals, is the philosophy of high impact training and success. I call it 'the mental software'.

Just like the most expensive computer systems, which are only as good and as useful as the software programs installed on them, it is essential that our mental software is the right one for the job in hand.

Let's move on to Chapter 2 and journey through the world of power thinking and key attitude strategies for remarkable changes in fortune and personal achievement. I can tell you now, once again from personal experience, that whatever the mind of a person can conceive and believe, he or she can surely achieve.

The SMART trainer's summary of Chapter 1

In summary, you have covered and learnt the following key factors that will help you achieve Beyond Traditional Training status. You have:

- learnt the danger of self-delusion;
- discovered that objective feedback is crucial;
- discovered that to know is to grow;
- decided to make allowances for others' poor feedback;
- become a feedback junkie;
- discovered other sources of feedback to use;
- understood how feeling exposed is a myth;
- explored the key area of reality versus self-perception;
- learnt that a successful life is an attitude thing – developing the right one.

Notes

1. Chapters 4 and 8 list the key SMART questions and show you great examples of evaluation questions that give you quality feedback.
2. Chapter 9 explores training-room confidentiality in more detail.
3. Part Three looks into this critical area with extreme frankness and amusing examples of 'how not to' do it.

2

UPGRADING YOUR MENTAL SOFTWARE FOR SUCCESS

'Formal education will make you a living, self-education can make you a fortune.'

(Jim Rohn)

Your learning objectives in this chapter

By the end of this chapter you will have learnt how your:

- current attitude towards training could be preventing you from achieving your full potential;
- current mental software can be easily and successfully upgraded;
- future thinking habits and actions can propel you into the 'beyond' training zone.

CREATURES OF HABIT

Who helped you get dressed this morning? One of the first things to realize is that we are all creatures of habit. Over 80 per cent of our daily tasks are carried out on autopilot, or in other words through our habits of behaviour – the way we dress, the way we walk, the way we talk and most importantly, the way we think. What are your current thinking habits? Are they working for you or against you? Our mindset[1] can be our biggest obstacle to success. For example:

> Who the hell wants to hear actors talk? (Harry Warner, 1927)
>
> There is no likelihood that man can ever tap the power of the atom. (Robert Millikan, 1923)
>
> Sensible and responsible women do not want to vote. (Grover Cleveland, 1927)
>
> Heavier-than-air flying machines are impossible. (Lord Kelvin, 1895)

As you can see from these few examples, our main enemy is mindset. When you hear or see something that conflicts with your current beliefs or values, you are likely to be dismissive of it. You will not even attempt to try to understand it; you will just brush it aside. This is known as 'cognitive dissonance'. This dissonance causes you discomfort, so you will either justify your present beliefs/behaviour or you will distort the new information in front of you so that it no longer challenges your 'world view'.

The dieticians and doctors tell us that we are what we eat. I can believe that, to a certain extent. Eat a load of lardy food and eventually you start to look a little lardy and you begin to feel a little lardy.

You need to realize right now that you are what you think. Think small, you'll talk small, you'll act small and you'll be small. Is that what you really want? It is essential to understand that to become a SMART trainer who operates Beyond the Traditional way you must keep an open mind and positive attitude at all times.

Before you run away with the idea that this is just going to be another chapter on positive thinking, think again. Positive thinking is OK, but you have to progress beyond that. Positive thinking is the junior school of success teaching. That's why they make those junior school desks and chairs so small, so you won't fit them as an adult. Positive thinking is fine, but without some positive action, it just remains as static, one-dimensional words on a page.

When I run my 'Success for Life' workshops I always ask the following two questions: 'Hands up who wants to be successful?' and 'Hands up who wants to be wealthy?' Guess how many hands go up. Yes, all of them. I then ask, 'Hands up all those who are currently studying success or wealth?' Now guess how many hands go up. Yes, right again – none.

When you decided to become a trainer, whether as an employee in an organization's training department or as an independent training consultant, you began to study your chosen craft. Sure, your company would have put you on a series of training courses to teach you the fundamentals (I hope) and you would have sat in on a number of other trainers' courses, to get a feel for how its done. You would have read some books. You studied the subject. It doesn't matter what example I use, if you wanted to become 'something' or do something you studied it.

Everyone I have ever come across, without exception, has wanted to become successful, yet not one of them was consciously studying the art of becoming successful. Why?

The brainwashing starts early

Habits of the mind, thinking habits, are long since ingrained by parents, teachers, peers and whoever else we chose to listen to. They all told us, either directly or indirectly, that success is something that just happens to other people. And then only if they're lucky. They were in the right place at the right time. They had the lucky breaks. They were born into it, or with it, whatever 'it' was.

We were exposed to this repeated process of mental indoctrination until it became, quite painlessly and quite silently, ingrained into our thinking patterns. By the time we were young adults, the belief was complete. The principles of propaganda are based on the same process. People will believe something to be true if they have heard it enough times regardless of the message source and facts.

ASSESSING YOUR CURRENT MENTAL SOFTWARE

What are your current thinking habits? How much limitation do they put on you? Would you be interested in exploring the possibility of removing your limitations?

Allow me to take you on a mental management audit where together we can explore how our thinking can really change the way we work, rest and play. And all without having to purchase that well-known chocolate bar.

A quick way to assess your current thinking habits is to consider how well you react to new ideas and methods. This is not always that easy, considering the problem of self-delusion, discussed in Chapter 1. It is well worth the effort to discover this though. Your thinking habits control your life.

Optimists have all the luck!

Would you consider yourself an optimist or a pessimist? Most people tend to go for the optimist tag or say that they are cautious rather than pessimistic. How cautious are you? Are you terrified of taking a risk? What do you consider to be a risk? Trying out something new in the training room can prove just too risky for many trainers. Unfortunately, this undermines not only their teaching impact but also the impact of all other trainers who follow them.[2]

Identify your restrictive thinking habits

No doubt you are aware of the comfort zone syndrome, where people stay with the actions, places and people they know well and feel at ease with. This is no good for the SMART trainer who aspires to greater achievements.

'Progress' is the SMART trainer's battle cry. If you're wallowing around in your comfort zone, as nice and secure as that may feel, you are just standing still. Standing still professionally in today's crazy world of accelerating change is professional suicide. Don't do it!

Become a student with attitude

A delegate on one of my Success for Life workshops came up to me after the workshop had finished. He asked me various questions about starting out as a consultant, improving his lifestyle, and becoming successful and wealthy. I asked him how much wealth he would like. He answered, 'Enough to get by.'

I was curious, so I asked him if he wanted to reward his hard work and dedication with anything along the way as he developed his own consultancy business. Why yes! A bigger house, a nicer car, better holidays. I told him that he would probably never achieve any of those if his wealth goal was based on 'enough to get by'. He looked a little puzzled until I explained to him that while his focus was on just earning enough to get by, then sub-consciously as soon as that 'enough' was reached his internal motivation would close down.[3]

Mysteries of the mind

Just like Jim Rohn, one the all-time greats on personal development strategies, I now know that there are certain things in life that are 'mysteries of the mind'. I don't know why certain things happen, I just know that they do. I used to spend a lot of time worrying and wondering about these things. The only thing I discovered was that it was a waste of my valuable time and my mental energy.

The way to make a success of your chosen profession and to become a SMART trainer who operates consistently Beyond Traditional Training methods is to become a student. This was my greatest discovery and my key to freedom – career freedom, work freedom, financial freedom. I can tell you now, before I became a student I was not free.

Become a student of what?

It is just like management skills. Let me explain. I run a six-day management skills programme which is split into two programmes of three days apiece. There is a period of some 6 to 10 weeks between the two programmes and the same delegates stay together to attend both. The first three-day programme is entitled 'Managing Yourself', the second, 'Managing Others'.

It is much more difficult and less effective to manage other people if you haven't first been taught how to manage yourself effectively. And so it is with trainers. To give the best to your students you must be a student first and foremost. Remember, all personal development and learning is continuous. SMART trainers never say, 'I now know all there is to know.'

WHY YOU NEVER GET PAID FOR YOUR TIME

The best advice I have ever received was during my self-study, way back in the early days of my development. That advice, which I religiously action at all times, was this: 'Learn to work harder on yourself than you do on your job.' I realized that working hard on my job would make me a living, but working hard on myself could earn me a fortune. And I'm not just talking about money here. When I count my fortune it also includes reputation, respect, credibility and know-how.

Where money is concerned most people don't fully appreciate just how it all works. You see, people get paid according to the value they bring to the market place. As a trainer I knew that the more value I could create for my delegates and for my clients through the training courses that I designed and delivered, the more enjoyment I would derive from it and the more they were likely to pay me.

After almost five years as an independent Peak Performance Specialist I know this to be true. You don't get paid for the time you put in, you get paid for the value you produce in that time. Here's an example.

A consultant was called into a company to solve a recurring problem with a production machine. It had stopped working once again and no one employed by the company could get it to work, so they called in an independent consultant.

He came in and spent the best part of a day examining the faulty machine, testing and checking his way all around the inert piece of equipment, asking the managers probing questions, then checking and testing some more. Finally he let out a gleeful 'ah-ha!', placed a chalk cross on one of the machine's panels, then went to his toolbox, pulled out a medium-weighted hammer, and gave the machine a measured whack. It kicked into life, and worked like it did when new.

The managers were delighted, thanked the consultant and told him to send in his invoice for swift payment.[4] The invoice duly arrived, but the managers were sent reeling in shock. The consultant wanted £1,000 for barely a day's work. The managers decided to query this as they thought it most excessive for the time spent working on their machine.

The managers called the consultant who listened to their query with patience. He let them finish and then told them he would send them a breakdown of the invoice. The next day they received the amended invoice, and it read:

> For time spent working on the machine = £100
> For knowing where to hit the machine = £900
> Total = £1,000.

We are all paid for what we know and how we use it. It comes back to that 'knowledge is strength' myth. Here's proof that it is the use of knowledge that is really profitable.

Once I learnt this it turned my life around. I suddenly began to see what it was really all about. I began to truly appreciate what it was like to be a delegate, and as a delegate, what it was that I wanted to experience on a training course or workshop.

How can you begin to deliver what your delegates want from a training experience if you have little or no appreciation of their needs and wants? And remember, wants are far more powerful motivators than needs. I'll give you a quick example. I may need to go to the gym on a regular basis in order to keep fit and healthy, but I don't want to so I'll find an excuse not to go – that sort of thing.

There are people who truly believe that they know all there is to know about their chosen profession. They have been doing 'the job' for many years; what else is there to learn? Over the years I have come across many managers with this attitude problem. If only they knew how much it holds them back. I would have managers say to me, 'I've been the manager of this department for 20 years. I know the job inside out and back to front. What else could I possibly learn?' Without realizing it, they had just described their comfort zone. Sadly, they were self-delusional. They didn't have 20 years' experience as a manager of their department. They had one year's experience repeated 20 times, not the same thing at all by any stretch of the imagination.

There are trainers just like this. They have been training the same subject for many years to a similar sea of faces. It ceased to be a challenge many years ago, but it's nice and comfortable, an easy little earner. Preparation is always minimal because they've done it so many times, the routines never change, the pace never changes, the outcome never changes – it's a habit. Habits are repeated actions carried out sub-consciously, on autopilot. The training is a long-established habit. And it's achingly boring.

The delegates sit there, in their polite British way. After an hour or less, they begin to suffer from TEGO. (Trainers love acronyms; this one stands for The Eyes Glaze Over.)

REMAINING CONSCIOUSLY COMPETENT

All trainers know the four stages of learning:

1. unconsciously incompetent;
2. consciously incompetent;
3. consciously competent;
4. unconsciously competent.

Training through habit belongs in Stage 4. This is not a good stage to be in while you are training, either before the course, while in preparation mode, or during delivery. I know it sounds obvious, but so many 'professional' trainers do it.

We are all human so it is easy to slip into this mode when undertaking a long repetitious training job, and that's why attitude and managing your thinking is so important. And that's why it is so important to become a student of life, people and the way we think.

It really is imperative that you become a student of your own attitude, behaviour and profession. How you think is how you are judged. It's governed by one of the universal laws,[5] the law of cause and effect, more commonly known as 'sowing and reaping'.

I network with a large number of consultants, both training and non-training, and I know that by practising this simple to implement process I receive a great deal more than I give out, and I give a great deal out. There are some people that I come across who falsely believe that they should receive before they give. This can never work because it comes in the same category as investment. The fundamental principle of investment is that you must invest in something first in order to receive a payback later. The takers in life are always moving on to new people, because people soon discover that they are not good people to be around and therefore remove them from their circle of influence.

BEHAVIOUR BREEDS BEHAVIOUR

Behaviour really does breed behaviour. You may well be aware of this truism already, yet you may not accept or acknowledge it consciously right now. I can tell you, quite categorically, that you will receive the type of behaviour and feedback from your course delegates as befits your attitude and behaviour towards them. It cannot be any other way because it is a universal law. It is worth mentioning here that in an ever-changing world, the universal laws are the only constant.

This is a good place to begin your studies. Study people's behaviour. Raise your awareness of how people react to others in relation to their behaviour towards them. This is very rewarding because it can teach you so much about the psychology of people very quickly.

SMART trainers have their finger on the pulse when it comes to reading people and assessing what their wants are. There is a mass of great material on the subject of psychology of learning, motivation and individual achievement. Begin to study it and become a serious student.

SMART trainers leave nothing to chance. They research their specialist field thoroughly. And while you may have a number of specialist fields your number one speciality will always be the same – people. And the number one person should always be you. To some people this may appear to be a selfish perspective, but in reality it is anything but. Let me share with you another example. To quote from the great Jim Rohn, 'No one respects the mother who becomes a martyr to her family. Pity the mother who turns herself into a martyr for she gains only contempt.' She falsely believes that she is there to do no more than take care of her family, at the expense of her own welfare and wellbeing.

Over the years I have discovered through my self-study that the most sensible and constructive perspective is as follows: 'I'll take care of me so that I can take care of you, if you take care of you so that you can take care of me.' That makes a whole lot more sense. If I fail to take care of my health and wellbeing then I become incapable of being useful to anyone, even myself, and that is not good self-management. And it is not good for the people I care for.

ALWAYS BEGIN WITH YOURSELF

This is where the process of upgrading your mental software must start – your current attitude and perspective towards your life and all aspects within it, and of course your beliefs. Do you have a scholar mentality or a victim mentality?

The scholar, who you are destined to now become, sees an unwelcome outcome as a lesson. A victim sees it as just more bad luck. Your beliefs determine your actions regarding yourself and your behaviour towards others. Beware! Just because they are your beliefs don't be fooled into thinking that they always serve your best interests.

The quality control of your life, your work and your training is governed by how you think. Everything must pass through it. And the best way that I have discovered to ensure maximum quality is through my philosophy.

Begin by creating your own philosophy

What is your philosophy? Do you have one? Is it the best one you could have? My philosophy used to be, 'Live for today, don't worry about tomorrow.' I soon learnt how shortsighted that was.

Live in the moment, enjoy the moment, and be there while it's happening. You have to be realistic though, for every tomorrow will surely become the today that you now face. Being casual about your future will always result in casualties.

You must have a sound philosophy, a primary aim to focus on and travel towards. This is the first and most critical step in the whole process of upgrading your mental software. You must be crystal clear about this point if you want to be a trainer who consistently operates 'beyond' the traditional fringe of training and development, and a trainer who commands great respect from your peers and participants on your training events. A trainer who earns what you are really worth, then.

THE ROUTE TO 'BEYOND' STARTS HERE

At the beginning of this book I said that I would start with the end in mind. The end result is you training as a SMART trainer in the Beyond Traditional Training process.

You will only move forward, and at the best possible pace, if your philosophy is sound. Once this is established other factors begin to gather momentum for your benefit.

Your philosophy will shape your attitude, which in turn will create new behaviours and, with repetition, produce new thinking habits. You need to replace any poor or suspect thinking habits as quickly as possible. To help you create your own philosophy and primary aim I will share mine with you. This is something that you will need to give some thought to. Get ideas down on paper.[6] Then play around with various ideas based on your vision of what you want to become. Here is my vision, which helped me shape my current plan:

> My key aim is to rid the world of bad trainers by creating more good ones and re-directing the bad ones. I want to become a world authority on personal development. I want to be recognized as the most focused and determined Peak Performance Specialist who will inspire people to make the necessary changes to their current attitudes and habits. I want to touch people's lives in a positive and constructive way. I want to help people take control of their own destiny. I want to help people work smarter. I want to teach people the methods to realize their true potential.
>
> I want to create and run my own Human Potential Centre so that I can train people in the correct thinking habits and behaviours for total success.

The belief I have and the attitude I communicate to clients and delegates alike is always, 'Your success is my success.' This will always remain true, for if you focus on making the people you are working with as successful as possible then success will always come back to you.

In a nutshell, my philosophy of life is really very simple. I want to do great things for others and I want great things for myself. And the time I realized that it could become a reality was when I discovered 10 words, all containing just two letters, during my own self-development. Those 10 words are:

> If it is to be, it is up to me.

Get rid of your blame list

My philosophy used to be faulty. Before I discovered these key elements, which catapulted me to the 'beyond' zone of training and development, and which will do the same for you too, I had a poor outlook on life.

I had a blame list as long as your arm. If my training courses were not so well received then I blamed the delegates, the venue, the hotel staff. If my finances were none too good then I blamed the bank, interest rates, inflation, taxes and the government. I blamed just about everyone. I learnt how wrong that was. Since I upgraded my mental software all those years ago, I became the much sought-after trainer I am today, successful and financially secure.

So what changed?

Today I can honestly say that the types of delegates who attend my courses are about the same as they were all those years ago. The hotels are about the same. The government is about the same, interest rates are about the same, taxes are about the same, and inflation is about the same. So what changed? I changed. I changed my thinking. I amended my attitude and reaped the rewards. And you can do the same.

If you have a blame list then vow to throw it away today, because it will only hinder your progress. Whatever you blame will control you. It is time to move beyond blame and to take responsibility for your own development and progress to become a SMART trainer.

By investing in my own development as an individual and a trainer I learnt the SMART route to successful training, which is preferable to the HARD route. Work long and hard, acting the hero with scant regard for your own welfare, wellbeing and progress. I have heard it many times: 'Invest in my own development. Huh, if only I had the time.'

I'm telling you now you cannot afford not to invest in your own growth. Believe me on this one: SMART beats HARD into a cocked hat every time. I have tried both, so I speak on good authority. For the record, the HARD acronym means:

Heroic
Action
Retards
Development.

Let us now prepare ourselves for Chapter 3. This is where we will explore the SMART questions we need to ask ourselves in order to establish firm foundations on which to build our Beyond Traditional Training plan.

There's nothing new in the world of training

Feel free to use my ideas as a catalyst for your own. As all trainers know, there is nothing new in training. I remember attending an Allan Pease seminar on communication and body language some years back. There was an audience of almost 100 for the morning session. Among the first words Allan spoke to the audience were, 'Hands up all the trainers here.' Over half the audience raised their hands. 'Ah-ha!' he exclaimed, taking out a pen and small notebook from inside his jacket as he furtively glanced around the sea of bemused faces, 'Material thieves.' He was of course absolutely right; most of the trainers even scribbled that line into their notebooks.

Whenever you can, avoid wasting time re-inventing the wheel. All training material is either recycled, revamped, restyled, rewritten or just plain copied straight as it is. Your time is a precious commodity that can never be replaced, so don't be careless with it.

So, if there's no new material out there for us trainers then what is critical is that there is an abundance of new thinking, fresh thinking or as I like to call it, 'thinking outside the box'.

From philosophy to focus

Once you have a working draft of your philosophy, you will most likely want to fine-tune it a few times as you develop your SMART trainer plan.[7] This will help you to clarify what attitude changes you will need to make in order to qualify for entry into the 'beyond' training zone.

KNOW YOUR PRIMARY AIM

Do you know your primary aim? If not, we'll get you one. Your primary aim is essential; without it your plan has no support for its structure. Your primary aim is, in essence, your backbone, where all levels and all branches of your overall plan are fed.

In order to establish your primary aim and then build the foundations of your overall plan you need to ask yourself a series of SMART questions. Through this process you will begin to re-programme your mental software so that you can operate in the 'beyond' zone with relative ease. I will take you through these in Chapter 3, which, as you will discover, is interactive, so make sure you have a pen or pencil ready.

The SMART trainer's summary of Chapter 2

In summary, you covered and learnt the following key factors that will help you achieve Beyond Traditional Training status:

- you are a creature of habit;
- brainwashing starts early;
- assess your current mental software;
- identify your restrictive thinking habits;
- become a student with attitude;
- why you never get paid for your time;
- become consciously competent;
- behaviours breed behaviour;
- always begin with yourself;
- creating your own philosophy – Part I;
- get rid of your blame list;
- there's nothing new in the world of training.

Notes

1. Link forward to Chapter 10 where you will find more information about mindsets.
2. I explain and demonstrate this in more detail in Chapter 5.
3. Questions that are put to work by your sub-conscious mind are explored in Chapter 12.
4. You're right; the consultant didn't believe this either.
5. There are many universal laws, which I will take you through in Chapter 8.
6. Peak performers always 'think in ink'.
7. Chapter 4 will take you through a step-by-step personal development process.

3

THE CRITICAL QUESTIONS ESSENTIAL FOR BECOMING A SMART TRAINER

'We must learn to apply all that we know so that we can attract all that we want.'

(Jim Rohn)

Your learning objectives in this chapter

By following this chapter's directions, ideas and suggestions you will have learnt how:

- creating powerful questions will guarantee you real progress and ultimate success;
- to compose SMART questions that work every time;
- to decide on a powerful primary aim and vision that will motivate you like never before.

UNDERSTANDING THE REAL POWER OF QUESTIONS

Everybody that I have ever come across, both in a professional capacity and in social settings, has always preferred action to apathy.

Before we get into the detail of critical questions and the role they play in shaping our performance, I will first share with you some important information, facts and examples of why asking SMART questions, as opposed to DUMB[1] questions, needs to be learnt.

Questions are the essence of relationships. They build rapport, allow us to gather information and to assess the situation so that we may make decisions that affect others and ourselves. And most importantly, in a positive way.

In general people don't pay enough attention to the questions they ask other people, and they don't pay enough, if any, attention to the questions they ask themselves. In fact, when you think about this for a while, you soon realize that people can be roughly divided into two categories: those who ask too many questions (the curious child comes to mind here) and those who never ask questions but just speak *at* you or never speak at all unless spoken to.

If you are to become a professional who wants to consistently perform at your personal best[2] then you need to realize that your own personal development plan, which you must follow to achieve that aim, will only be as good as the questions you ask yourself.

In Chapter 2 you looked at thinking habits and questions as playing a major part in forming those habits of the mind. Now, are you generating good habits or compounding bad habits? Let's have a look.

WHO TALKS TO YOU THE MOST?

When I ask delegates this question they very rarely give me the right answer first time. Their immediate thoughts go to their boss or partner, or parents if they still live at home. Of course the one and only correct answer to that question is *you*.

You speak to yourself incessantly. Everybody does. We can all talk the hind legs off the proverbial donkey when it comes to internal chit-chat. If we bombarded others with the barrage of nit-picking and negative observations that we often hit ourselves with we'd drive them loopy. We'd never have any friends or any decent relationships. There are some people who actually do this to others, and let's be honest, if we can we avoid them. We guard ourselves against their negativity and soul-destroying outpourings. When it's someone else, you can. However, it's impossible to get away from yourself – at least I haven't been able to master that one yet.

THE ANSWER IS YES, NOW WHAT'S THE QUESTION?

The simple information that this answer gives us is that the question was a closed one. Closed questions are those useful questions we fire at people if we want to gather key facts about them quickly. However, they're not very helpful if we want to gain a deeper insight into their feelings and motivations.

For more detail we need to ask open questions, but they need to be SMART open questions. The classic DUMB question, in my opinion, is the interview one that most interviewers kick off with when recruiting people: 'Can you tell me about yourself?' While this question is technically a closed question, the answer is always delivered as if an open question had been asked, due to the fact that all interviewees are expecting this question, because it is now such a cliché. Also, everyone who is being interviewed for a job, even if it is for the first time, instinctively knows exactly what the interviewer is after at this early point in the proceedings.

The main reason I consider this question to be a DUMB one is that it is not specific enough. Where does the poor interviewee begin? With their childhood, first job or what they've done over the last six months? Also, it is unimaginative and lazy.

Questions play an important part in our lives, yet most people don't realize this. I will share with you a couple of quick examples and then I will get you to focus on your main objectives for this chapter.

First, questions are critical in building rapport with people. Now we all know how powerful rapport can be when it comes to gaining another person's respect, support and co-operation. SMART trainers understand the psychology of this. After all, they have made a point of studying the importance of questions when establishing new relationships. Remember every training course that you run begins with you having to establish the parameters of your relationship and building a strong rapport as quickly as possible. Without this your job, which is to convince and persuade your audience that the skills, strategies and techniques that you are sharing with them should be acted on as soon as they return to work,[3] is unlikely to be complete. All SMART trainers work to the policy of making delegate co-operation as easy as possible.

Even in social settings we want people to like us and be influenced by us. Yet, in order to do this we decide that the best strategy is to use the 'Look at me aren't I wonderful' technique.[4] This never works, for it only fools the extremely gullible, and they are not really the best people you want to be attracting into your life if you want to achieve great success.

I work with a fellow consultant, Peter Brooks, who has devised a fantastic workshop for both business and schools called WOW! (World of Work!). It was designed initially for sixth-formers and graduates who were working hard at getting to grips with the real world. Basically what they needed was social and communication skills. As both Peter and I specialize in communication skills we would take the students through a series of participative workshop sessions. We wanted to train them in the art of communicating so that they could present themselves to the big bad world of work without appearing a complete nerd or sociopath.

The classic errors made by most young men were in four areas:

1. Lack of questions in the first instance.
2. Badly composed questions in the second.
3. The 'let's talk about me' syndrome.
4. No time, inclination or ability to listen to the other person.

USING SMART TRAINER SKILLS TO DESIGN THE WOW! WORKSHOP

Peter and I both realized, being SMART trainers, that the first question the delegates would be asking themselves (as you recall we all talk to ourselves the most) would be the classic WIIFM? or what's in it for me? We knew that if we didn't answer this question quickly for them we would struggle to keep their attention long enough to teach them anything. So we approached it from the angle that would appeal to the vast majority of testosterone-packed 18-year-olds: how to successfully chat up the person of your desires. This was something they could all relate to, with all but a few naturals having suffered their fair share of rejection.

We told the story of a handsome young man who was very sporty, fit and popular with his friends. However, when it came to trying to get a date with the opposite sex, he failed miserably every time. Why? He would approach the young lady confidently enough, drink in hand, and sidle up to her and introduce himself. She would be looking pleasantly surprised. She had noticed him watching her for some time and thought that he looked cute. He would then ask her name. All OK so far. I mean, he's even got a question in quite early, but then it would turn against him. He would follow up his first question with a brief nod to acknowledge her name (he never spoke it) and then launch into his own life story. 'I'm the captain of the rugby team, you know.' 'I'll be going to Oxford in the spring term.' 'I've just been selected to represent the college at the next triple-A track event.' It was all I, I, I. After a few minutes of this the poor girl begins to show signs of TEGO. He has now got no chance.

No control equals no chance

Of course the reason that he has no chance is because he has no control over the conversation. Whoever asks the questions controls the moment. The person you are trying to impress doesn't want to hear your voice, droning on; they want to hear their own sweet dulcet tones. If you're not consciously asking prepared questions then you just babble on about yourself. Why else do you think that politicians virtually always answer a question with another question that they then answer themselves? It's a simple tactic that allows them to regain control of the situation and answer a question that they have prepared earlier. Good political interviewers don't let them get away with this of course. A good way to study the craft of SMART question techniques is by watching programmes such as 'Newsnight'.

So asking questions – SMART questions remember – is essential in order to gain important information that you can either store for later retrieval, or use to strengthen your present position.

The reason the student in our example didn't ask any questions and became besotted with his own importance was very human. People love to talk about themselves. We all long to be able to share our triumphs and achievements with our friends, family – in fact anyone who will listen. We can use this simple psychological factor to our advantage in both professional and social settings. And that's the beauty of these skills: they're easy to implement and you get ample opportunities to practise. Practise at work, at home, while out with friends, when meeting strangers.

This is how it works. Knowing that people like talking about themselves, we prepare ourselves and consciously design it so that they get the opportunity. We ask them a series of questions that will allow them to share with you the things they love to do, places they've been, successes they've achieved. We listen actively.

Oops! This is where most people go wrong because they haven't realized just how difficult a skill active listening really is. Active listening is a conscious activity; we cannot successfully implement this skill while on autopilot.

THE DIFFERENCE BETWEEN WHAT WE NEED AND WHAT WE'VE BEEN TAUGHT

Interestingly, when we communicate, these are the skills we use and the amount of time we spend using them:

Listening	45%
Talking	30%
Reading	16%
Writing	9%

When we then look at how much time was spent on teaching us these skills when we were at school, we begin to see where the problem lies. At school the amount of time spent teaching us the key communication skills were:

Writing	45%
Reading	35%
Speaking	20%
Listening	0%

It's a matter of speed

Listening skills are something we all have to work on because nobody has ever bothered to teach us. Another key factor concerns speeds. We speak, on average, about 150 to 200 words a minute. We think, again on average, about 800 words a minute. This is because we tend to think in pictures, concepts and comprehension, so the words per minute are an equivalent example. You can see that a conflict exists here: 200 words per minute, talking; 800 words per minute, thinking. Now, the problem lies in two key areas. Number one is our strong desire to be the one speaking; number two is that we are thinking at 800 words per minute of the things we will be saying as soon as the person talking shuts up.

THE ACTIVE LISTENING TECHNIQUE THAT ALWAYS WORKS

Here is a little technique that will help you to practise active listening. After you have asked the question that allows the other person to share with you his or her good fortune, you give 100 per cent of your attention while he or she is speaking, and slow down your thinking speed. You can do this quite easily by following, at the same pace in your head, exactly what he or she is saying. Then you really do hear all that is being said, and you can prove that you were actually listening by asking a follow-up question, either a clarification or probing question. This creates positive feelings towards you and is part of the process, which I will take you through later on in your workshop, for building rapport with your delegates in the SMART trainer way.

A word of caution at this point would be useful. When you first start practising this great technique, make sure you are not moving your lips while you follow the answer to your question. People will begin to find this quite unnerving, and put you down as someone best avoided.

Questions always force people to do two things:

1. Think about what you have just said.
2. Give a response to your question.

When I'm training people in a new conceptual skill, such as the psychology of motivating others, I need to help them to explore territory outside of their normal mindset. People's beliefs can be very ingrained and hard to change, so asking questions can be a powerful tool in helping them see things from a different viewpoint. Once they know that I want them to respond with a thought or feeling on that subject (their cue is the fact that it's a question) then they must think about the subject from the angle that I have highlighted through my question. In other words, through my SMART questions I assertively challenge their current belief and mindset on that subject.

We can use this same process when asking questions of ourselves. If we are to successfully upgrade our mental software then we must start by challenging our own current beliefs and checking that our own current mindset is appropriate for the situation we are now in and for any future circumstances that we want to create for ourselves.

Is your current mindset hindering your progress? Let's check it out. First I'll give you a quick example. A good time management question to ask yourself as you work on a task would be, 'Is this the most effective use of my time right now?' If you answer yourself honestly you will know whether you need to do one of two things:

- You answer YES. Then you carry on working on the task.
- You answer NO. Then you stop what you are currently doing and check against your list of prioritized tasks what you *should* be doing and start work on that.

If this sounds easy, that's because it really is. In life people, as a general rule, tend to make things far more complex than they need to be. We often come across possible or potential solutions and think that they could never work because they seem far too simple or easy. We drive ourselves to distraction searching for complicated answers when most of the time it's the most straightforward process of all.

Here are some more SMART self-questions:

- How could my current training delivery be improved?
- In what more exciting ways could I design my training sessions?
- If I were a delegate on the courses I run, what would make me sit up and really take notice?
- If I were a delegate on the courses I run, would I be impressed with what I saw?
- If I were a delegate on the courses I run, would I be impressed with what I heard?
- If I were a delegate on the courses I run, would I be impressed with the manner in which it was spoken?
- As a delegate, what would I have had to experience on a training course that would make me want to come back for more?
- As a delegate, what would I have had to experience on a training course that would make me go back to my workplace and sing its praises?

These self-questions should be treated in the same way as if someone else were posing them to you. In other words, you think it through and then respond. Make sure that you 'think in ink' by writing down your answers for the record and future development.

As a delegate, what *would* make you sit up and really take notice? What's stopping you from implementing that in your own courses so that your delegates experience the same thing? In reality absolutely nothing is stopping you. However, your current mindset may be saying, 'What works for me wouldn't work for them, because surely everyone is different?' This, like all restrictive mindsets, is based on assumption. And assumption is lazy communication practice, as we will explore in more detail in Part Two of your workshop.

ALL DELEGATES WANT THE SAME TWO THINGS REGARDLESS OF THE SUBJECT TAUGHT

'Surely not!' I hear you saying. 'How can delegates being taught Communication Skills want the same things as those being taught Manual Handling Techniques?' This is a common error in viewpoint. You are thinking this because you are confusing training content with training outcome. Let me explain.

As we know, *training content* such as the subject information is the nuts and bolts of the training course itself. The relevant data includes the examples, the visual aids, the exercises and the supporting materials. *Training outcome* is part of the training deliverables, which can only happen if the key question is addressed right at the start of the training event.

Delegates tend to ask themselves, sometimes consciously but most often sub-consciously, two questions very quickly on learning that they are to attend a training course. The first question is always, why me?[5] This is followed up, between learning of the upcoming course and sitting there, arms crossed, in front of you on the morning, with, yes that's right, the question, 'What's in it for me?' It is important to bear in mind that because the delegates don't believe that there is anything in it for them in attending, they are saying mentally and through their body language, 'I don't want to be here.'

Now, if you fail to answer this question for them they never really get fully involved in the events that follow the delegate introduction session. They remain stuck in that 'I don't want to be here' mode. This is not good for you the trainer or your other delegates. So the two critical pieces of information that every delegate wants to receive as soon as possible are:

1. The purpose of them being there.
2. The personal benefits they will receive from attending the training course.

SMART TRAINERS SELL IMPROVEMENT

Training is a selling game first and a vehicle for personal development and improvement second. This is not something that I have made up because it sounds like it might be a good theory. Put simply, the basics of human psychology apply here as they do to all other things in life. This is an important area to get right. And this is why SMART trainers study the psychology of people and their subsequent behaviours and apply the techniques and strategies regardless of the subjects taught.

Research tells us that people hate to be sold to, but that they do love to buy. On first reading this may seem like a contradiction, but it isn't. It's simply being human. The vast majority of people hate to feel that they are being manipulated and coerced into a series of actions decided for them by someone else, or in other words, being made to do something even if it is for their own good. This is something that goes right back to early childhood and has been rigorously practised ever since. For countless generations parents have advised their children not to do certain things or to do other things for their own good. For example:

> Don't smoke, it's very bad for you.
> Don't ride a motorcycle, they're really dangerous.
> You must stay on at school, it will help you get a better job.
> You don't want to be friends with that person, they're bad news.

And the list can go on. The parents were selling to their children. Their children, like all other human beings, hated being sold to and in the vast majority of cases did not heed their parents' advice and therefore did not buy. However, through the personal experience of trying these things out for themselves or discovering more about them another way, they bought the benefits and changed their behaviour accordingly.

Why? Because it was their own decision, made via their own realization after studying the facts as they experienced them.

SMART trainers know that delegates attending courses are very much the same. Your training events have to be geared to allowing the delegates the opportunity to discover benefits they will enjoy once they have mastered a few simple techniques and strategies. So, how do you this? Well it's kicked off with a few questions. This is an area that we will be exploring in some detail in Chapter 9. If you want to fast-forward to this chapter and read it out of sequence, it won't cause you any problems. For now though we will move on to the final part of this important foundation-building chapter.

QUESTIONS TO HELP YOU CREATE YOUR PRIMARY AIM AND VISION

Whenever I run my Success for Life workshops most of the people attending have the same difficulties in deciding what it is they would really like to do with their life – what they would like to earn their living doing and what they would like to become. This is simply because they are not asking themselves the right questions. In fact most of them don't ask any self-questions at all. The only statement they really make is one that has an outward focus, as in, 'I don't know what I want to do', as if I'm supposed to magic them the ideal career solution. And it is often said in a rather pathetic, whiney way, rather like bored children indoors on a rainy day where their mother won't let them out to play.

If you feel that you are on a road to nowhere it is because you have not taken yourself through the essential process of self-questioning for your personal purpose. The questions that I would get my Success for Life delegates to ask themselves would be along the following lines.

The first thing I get them to do is to imagine the following scenario. It is Saturday evening and they have just won the National Lottery jackpot of £5 million. I then ask them if they would still continue doing what they currently do for a living after they pick up their huge cheque. Bar the rare exception, everyone in the room says 'No way.'

The next question I ask them to give serious consideration to is the following: 'If money were no object, what would you choose to do because you really wanted to do it?' The answer (or answers in some cases) they give to this question becomes their starting point for their own Action for Success Plan.

Get your pen ready for the 12 critical questions.

Now if you are really serious about becoming a SMART trainer who wants to achieve Beyond Traditional Training status, let me ask you some questions. Please give honest and full answers in the boxes provided. You will be referring back to these when you work through Chapter 4's session on action planning.

1. Why did you get involved in training?

2. What do you want to achieve for others through the profession of training?

3. What do you want to achieve for yourself by being a trainer?

4. When you are delivering training, what do you consider you do that is above average standard in your performance?

5. Which training methods do you consider to be below average standard in your delivery performance?

6. Which elements of your training course design would you most like to improve?

7. Which elements of your current training delivery style would you most like to improve?

8. What do you think delegates most like about being trained by you?

9. What do you think delegates like least about being trained by you?

10. What are the most common type of problems you encounter with delegates during your training events?

11. What was the toughest delegate problem you have ever had to handle? And how did you handle it?

12. How much time do you currently invest in your own development (ie reading books, listening to audiobooks, attending seminars and training courses, etc)? Put some figures to your answers in terms of hours and money spent.

You will come back to your answers to these questions in Chapter 4 when I take you through a simple step-by-step SMART trainer's development plan. There you will be able to better and more quickly create the foundations of a powerful success strategy that you will be able to implement immediately.

Your primary aim, values and vision

Now you need to consider, again so that you can create your success strategy to quickly bring you the results that you desire, a series of critical questions that will enable you to draft your primary aim and personal values and vision. These, as you will come to realize if you don't already, are the cornerstones of your strategy. They allow you to determine the following key steps:

- what further knowledge you require;
- what further experience and practice you need;
- what actions you need to implement.

With this information at your disposal you will have a vehicle that will mobilize you to 'Massive Action' and it is the 'Massive Action' philosophy that will deliver you to your goals and of course your success as a SMART trainer who consistently operates at the high level of Beyond Traditional Training status.

To help you determine your own values for your strategy, here are two lists that you can use as a reference. They are known as 'Moving-Toward' values and 'Moving-Away-From' values:

- *Moving-Toward values:* love; success; freedom; intimacy; security; adventure; power; passion; comfort; health.
- *Moving-Away-From values:* rejection; anger; frustration; loneliness; depression; failure; humiliation; guilt; cynicism.

A quick word on values

Everyone is motivated by his or her emotions. We are either motivated away from something perceived as painful (either emotionally or physically) or we are motivated towards something that we perceive will bring us pleasure. Away motivators are the strongest and are the catalyst for change in our behaviours.

A typical example that applies to many people I know and once applied to me many years ago, would be concerning personal finances. For instance, you continue to spend more than you earn because spending gives you pleasure, a sense of power to have nice things and money in your pocket. The bills come in along with the bank statements and you ignore them and leave them unopened. They depress you and make you feel guilty and angry with yourself, so you move away from them.

This continues until your situation is so perilous (you are in real danger of losing your partner (loneliness, rejection), losing your house and job (humiliation and failure)) that you are moved to make some immediate changes in your circumstances. You seek help and begin to behave in a 'toward' way to ensure you safeguard your security, freedom, comfort and health.

Primary aim, values and vision questions – the next six key questions

13. What is most important to me in life?

14. What would I like to achieve in the field of training and development that would be considered genuinely for the good of others?

15. What would I like to achieve for myself as a training professional?

16. Where would I like to be in my career in five years' time?

17. Where would I like to be with my financial situation in five years' time?

18. What type of person would I like to become?

With these questions now answered, at least in draft form, we can move on to preparing the foundations of your action plan in the next session in Chapter 4.

The SMART trainer's summary of Chapter 3

In summary, you covered and learnt the following key factors that will help you achieve Beyond Traditional Training status:

- understanding the real power of questions;
- who talks to you the most;
- SMART and DUMB questions;
- communication skills we need versus what we were taught;
- the speed of talking compared to the speed of listening and thinking;
- the active listening technique that always works;
- all delegates want the same two things;
- SMART trainers sell development;
- the 12 critical questions for your self-development plan;
- the six key questions for your primary aim.

Notes

1. Another acronym, which stands for Dopey Utterings Meant to Baffle.
2. This is Peak Performance and can be experienced in Chapter 9.
3. This is the key element of giving your delegates and clients (or boss!) value for money. You will learn more about this in Chapter 11.
4. A great many traditional trainers work with this strategy, as you will discover in Chapter 6.
5. This is a question that usually doesn't even get answered, as it should be, by the delegate's manager.

4

PREPARING THE FOUNDATIONS OF YOUR ACTION PLAN – ACTION PLAN PART I

'Action will always be the key to greatness.'

(Jim Rohn)

Your learning objectives in this chapter

By following this chapter's directions, ideas and suggestions you will have learnt how:

- to launch yourself on to the path of SMART trainer status with the foundation of your Personal Development Plan;
- SMART questions give you control over your desired outcomes of your plan, your progress and any other situation that you may find yourself in;
- to create a step-by-step process of future achievement through a series of self-assessment inventories and development tools.

BEGIN WITH THE END IN MIND

To quote Dr Stephen Covey from his great work, *The Seven Habits of Highly Effective People*, begin with the end in mind for this is where it all begins, once you have decided that you want to improve; in other words, once you have decided to act. As it states at the beginning of this chapter, action will always be the key to greatness.

OK, you're ready to get into action so let's produce your initial template for future success in the SMART trainer league. You can do this through a series of questions you are going to ask yourself and answer with total honesty. I know that I don't need to emphasize this as you will already know that without honesty self-improvement cannot take place. If I link back to Chapter 1 and the dangers of self-delusion then I know that you can move on to the first draft of your self-improvement Action Plan.

WHERE AM I NOW?

To create a pathway of actions that you must carry out in order to achieve the status of a SMART trainer who consistently operates at the Beyond Traditional Training level, you need to establish where you are today.

Carefully read through the following list of questions. Besides being a great list of SMART questions that you can regularly refer to during future self-assessment sessions for your professional improvement, they will also prepare you for the questionnaire that follows:

- How passionately do you currently train?
- How energetically do you currently deliver input sessions?
- What level of participation do you put your delegates through?
- How creative is your course design?
- How much fun do you put into your training sessions?
- What is your current attitude towards training activities?
- How much time do you allow for course preparation?
- How flexible are you with regard to your training session timetable?
- How well do you answer questions from your delegates?
- How much time do you spend selling your credibility?
- How much time do you spend relaxing your delegates?
- What methods do you employ to keep delegates' interest and concentration levels high as your courses progress?

Now read through the questionnaire and score it with complete honesty. Show it how it really is, warts and all. I know this may make you feel a little uncomfortable, but it is for your own good. You can only benefit from a truly honest appraisal of your current performance standards.

Remember that no one else will see this unless you choose to share it; it is for your eyes only. Once you have a clear picture of where you are now, you can then decide to put yourself through the appropriate changes in order to increase your effectiveness.

YOUR MEASUREMENT OF PROGRESS

Once you have completed the following short questionnaire you will then complete your PEQ™. This stands for Personal Effectiveness Quotient and was developed by a fellow consultant, colleague and friend, Peter Thomson, who is head of Results International plc and the BBCTA (British Business Consultants and Trainers Academy).

The PEQ™ is a fantastic measurement tool that reveals so much about how well we are currently doing by employing the appropriate skills to our profession, and how much more we could achieve with some simple actions of improvement. The PEQ™ is also a great tool to use on training courses and workshops.

With this revealing and fun device you will be able to begin improving your impact on your training courses immediately. First though, you need to complete your self-assessment questionnaire.

SELF-ASSESSMENT INVENTORY

Complete the following questions as accurately as you can by shading in the bar to the score that truly applies to your performance.

1. How do you currently rate your training delivery impact within the following categories?

When I deliver my training sessions I… (create the following in my delegates)

Send them to sleep – generate some interest – get them leaning forward – make them keen and excited

1	2	3	4	5	6	7	8	9	10

2. How subdued or demonstrative are you when performing in front of delegates?

When presenting a training course the energy I display to my delegates is…

Static and monotone – slow and low volume – pacey and punchy – knock their socks off – WOW!

1	2	3	4	5	6	7	8	9	10

3. Following your introduction, do you explain how the current situation relates to your audience?

When opening my courses I consider selling the benefits of my audience attending as being…

Unheard of – pointless – unnecessary – a good idea – essential – critical

1	2	3	4	5	6	7	8	9	10

4. Before and during your training sessions how do you really feel?

Just before I begin and when delivering my training sessions I want to…

Be somewhere else – hurry up and finish – do the job well and go home – exceed their expectations

1	2	3	4	5	6	7	8	9	10

5. How do you observe your audience during your training delivery?

When I'm training I am looking for…

A friendly face – the next feed for a joke – signs of encouragement – early evidence of discomfort

1	2	3	4	5	6	7	8	9	10

How have you scored? The idea of this process is not to say that you're this good or this bad, but to determine how far away you are from achieving the high-scoring Beyond Traditional Training status. Do not judge yourself too harshly. I most certainly will not be judging you. One of the key points I make during the opening session of all my courses is that the training event the delegates are about to experience will be totally non-judgemental.

I want people to relax and really open up. The fewer barriers there are cluttering their minds, the more they will get out of the training and the more you, the trainer, will get out of the training. This is my key aim, with all that you will have read through, the practising of the strategies, techniques and processes contained within this book. As I stated earlier, I am taking you through a written version of my Train the Trainer Master Class programme. My aim is to coach you through to your desired goals.

Honest self-assessment

Now have a closer look at the scores in the five questions you have just answered. My guess is, you have tweaked a little bias into the scoring. This is totally understandable and expected. I now want you to reduce your scoring by two points for each question. I know it sounds harsh but it is for the best. I want you to become very successful at delivering your training courses and workshops and I know that in order to do that the process of self-development must be a little tough.

Rose-tinted glasses

I'm guilty of looking at the world through rose-tinted glasses at times, especially when it is at my own performance. Yes, singing our own praises is important at regular intervals, when deserved, but we also need to balance this for really effective self-improvement to take place.

If we never break the self-congratulatory cycle then complacency very quickly sets in and we revert back to our old friend, who we met back in Chapter 1: self-delusion. Of course, as I've said, we need this process to be balanced, so too much self-criticism should also be avoided. You don't want to lack any confidence and self-belief as a trainer, otherwise selling your credibility to your delegates becomes a tough uphill struggle.

Becoming self-effacing during reflective periods of personal improvement is allowed and necessary for your progress. In essence, this will ensure that you remain in the real world and also allow you to remain in the third stage of learning, which, as all SMART trainers know, is the best stage to operate from.

THE FOUR STAGES OF LEARNING

Every one goes through the four stages of learning, and all SMART trainers and apprentice SMART trainers will know these stages off by heart. Very briefly though, let us revisit them and explore them from the perspective of a trainer delivering important lessons to his or her audience.

Stage 1: Unconscious incompetence

You don't know that you don't know what you need to know to carry out the job in hand competently.

There are trainers I have come across on my travels who would fall into this category. Admittedly they are quite rare, but they do practise the art of delivering effective knowledge and skills transfer rather badly.

Unfortunately, there are some personnel officers and managers who also operate in this stage when dealing with training issues. The most difficult task is getting them to understand this. Decisions made on staff development, while working in stage one, can have a major impact on results, profits and staff morale and motivation.

I had a rather worrying experience when working for one client some years back. I was commissioned to run a series of skills workshops for newly promoted team leaders. Everything was arranged and my brief told me that the first of these training courses would begin at 9 am. Like all SMART trainers I like to turn up at least 90 minutes before the start, especially if I haven't been there before. I arrived at security and signed in and was directed to reception. I announced myself to the receptionist and obtained my pass. The receptionist then attempted to tell my contact, the Personnel Manager, that I was waiting in reception. However, he wasn't in work yet. Well it was only 7.45 am, so no need to panic.

While I waited I unloaded my materials and then went and parked my car. The receptionist continued to call my contact during this time.

I sat and waited. I read the company newsletters, the notice board. The receptionist kept trying his number. The time kept creeping on: 8.10 – 8.25 – 8.35 – 8.40. I was still sat there, surrounded by my materials, not knowing where the room was, what it was like and wondering how quickly I could set up the room.

At 8.50, just 10 minutes before the course was due to start, the Personnel Manager appeared and greeted me. Shaking my hand he said, 'I didn't expect you this early, the course doesn't start until 9.' After I had recovered from the shock of this blatant display of ignorance I mumbled that I like to spend a little time to set the room up and get things ready. He replied, 'Oh!' in a somewhat puzzled tone.

Stage 2: Conscious incompetence

Having attended a training course, read a book, experienced a SMART trainer's delivery style and impact, you become aware that you don't know as much as you believed you knew about the job or task in hand.

Initially this will unsettle you. This is quite normal so don't worry about it too much. However, you are to be congratulated because you can now progress towards the next stage and to relative safety. A light has clicked on and it can only get better from here, for you and your delegates. A period of learning and practice now takes place as you develop towards the third stage of learning.

Stage 3: Conscious competence

You now know that you know how it works and continue to work hard at making it happen to the right standards, continuously striving for excellence in the impact of your training delivery and knowledge. You also continue to better your performance through regular reviews, feedback sessions and skills and knowledge updates, refreshers and re-training.

Don't get too carried away. It is during this period, if you are not careful, that you can easily slip into the fourth stage of learning. Human beings, as we have already discussed, are creatures of habit. Habit becomes routine and routine changes into an ever-deepening rut. Before you know where you are you're performing, for the whole world to see (well, at least the delegates in front of you at the time), on autopilot.

Stage 4: Unconscious competence

Operating on autopilot for long periods is not the best option. OK, so on many occasions you can get away with it, but not forever. Besides, it's not good for your professional health or for the benefit and enjoyment of your delegates.

What causes you to dip into Stage 4?

Self-delusion is one of the causes of people slipping into Stage 4. They believe, incorrectly, that they are performing in Stage 3, competently and with professionalism. However, the reality is that familiarity really does breed contempt. By operating in Stage 4 we carry out tasks and actions without proper conscious thought. This makes us careless. And allowing ourselves to become careless means 'that we couldn't care less' about the impact of our actions.

The main problem with working in Stage 4 is that we carry out a certain number of acts subconsciously and are therefore unable to make the necessary checks for quality. Is this what we really want for our delegates or for our hard-earned reputations? Although it takes more effort we must work at remaining in Stage 3. As we raise our awareness we will catch ourselves as we slip into Stage 4. Don't be hard on yourself; just make the conscious effort to move back up to operating in conscious competence.

BUILDING ON THE FOUNDATION OF YOUR PERSONAL DEVELOPMENT PLAN (PDP)

You now know that you need to remain in Stage 3 in order to deliver your training at a constant level of quality. However, you also need to be adding to your knowledge and skill levels and the best way to do this is through questions, self-assessment and a step-by-step plan.

Your effectiveness as a trainer is determined by multiplying the effect of:

- How much you know.
- How well you use what you know.
- How often you use what you know.

For this process, you can use the PEQ™ format. You can determine the skills, knowledge and usage that you currently work to. You will then self-score this and calculate your current effectiveness quotient. Be aware that this will initially surprise you. Let's go through this now.

The questions

First, let's create a list of key skills that form the basis of SMART trainer competences. For ease and manageability we will choose 10, which in my opinion would be:

1. Active listening.
2. Questioning techniques.
3. Handling conflict and confrontation.
4. Building rapport (NLP, body language, communication).
5. Self-organization/self-management.
6. Negotiation techniques.
7. Influencing and persuasion skills.
8. Motivational techniques.
9. Facilitation skills.
10. Observation skills.

We can now answer three key questions:

1. How much knowledge do I have of this skill?
2. How well can I implement it?
3. How often do I use it?

Using the PEQ™ as a framework, you can measure your current effectiveness. You can do this now and use it as a personal development progress tracker as you develop and build your knowledge and skills over the coming months and years.

Figure 4.1 is an example of a completed PEQ™ grid for you to study. Have a look at how it works and then turn to the blank form in Figure 4.2 and complete a PEQ™ grid for yourself. For your first one use the same skill areas and score yourself with complete honesty. The scoring is self-correcting. So, when you try to determine a score for the knowledge dimension, you may find that when putting yourself through some skills training on that particular subject, you know more than

PERSONAL EFFECTIVENESS QUOTIENT

You achieve success in work and life by multiplying the effect of...

A) *How much* you know

B) *How well* you use what you know

C) *How often* you use what you know

Calculating your PEQ

Name:	*A*	*B*	*C*
Key	*How Much*	*How Well*	*How Often*
1. Active listening	7	6	8
2. Questioning techniques	8	8	8
3. Handling conflict/confrontatioh	6	6	7
4. Building rapport	7	6	6
5. Self-organization/management	7	5	7
6. Negotiation techniques	6	6	8
7. Influencing/persuasion skills	7	6	7
8. Motivational techniques	7	6	8
9. Facilitation skills	6	5	7
10. Observation skills	6	4	7
TOTAL	67	58	73
DIVIDE EACH TOTAL BY 10 *And then complete the measurement below*	6.7	5.8	7.3

Now calculate the following to find out your current overall Personal Effectiveness Quotient™ out of a possible 100%

Column A Total		Column B Total		Column C Total		Total Score	Divide by	PEQ Score
6.7	X	5.8	X	7.3	=	283.678	10	28.36%

Figure 4.1 *Personal Effectiveness Quotient – example*

PERSONAL EFFECTIVENESS QUOTIENT

You achieve success in work and life by multiplying the effect of...

A) *How much* you know

B) *How well* you use what you know

C) *How often* you use what you know

Calculating your PEQ

Name:	***A***	***B***	***C***
Key	***How Much***	***How Well***	***How Often***
1.			
2.			
3.			
4.			
5.			
6.			
7.			
8.			
9.			
10.			
TOTAL			
DIVIDE EACH TOTAL BY 10 *And then complete the measurement below*			

Now calculate the following to find out your current overall Personal Effectiveness Quotient™ out of a possible 100%

Column A Total		Column B Total		Column C Total		Total Score	Divide by	PEQ Score
	X		X		=		10	%

Figure 4.2 *Personal Effectiveness Quotient – for you to complete*

you originally gave yourself credit for. If this is the case then you can adjust the score accordingly in the next assessment you put yourself through.

As you can see in the example in Figure 4.1, even with these scores the overall effectiveness is just 28.6 per cent. Now, to put it into perspective, let us assume that you are being as effective as you currently are, on a day-to-day basis, with just 28.6 per cent PEQ™. Imagine what a modest improvement in all 10 skill areas over the three dimensions (how much, how well and how often) would do to your overall effectiveness as a trainer. And what's more, you now have a tool to measure your progress as you develop towards becoming a SMART trainer.

Now that you have familiarized yourself with the workings of the PEQ™ complete the blank grid for your own skill assessment. Remember to keep positive no matter how low the score comes out. If you get a particularly low score check that you haven't been too hard on yourself.

Using a benchmark

When I use this on my Personal Development workshops I get the delegates to use as a role model someone they admire for their high competency and effectiveness in the same skills that they want to develop.

Once they have chosen someone, I then get them to imagine that that person would have a score of nine in all dimensions and to use that as a benchmark. This then allows them to make a comparison with their own skill levels and to score their own accordingly.

This will give you a good starting base and enable you to create a foundation on which to build your personal development Action Plan. You will be able to learn the best ways of increasing your knowledge, ability and frequency of use in Chapter 11.

The personal SWOT analysis

Now that you have completed the questionnaires and your PEQ™, you can carry out a very simple yet highly effective personal SWOT analysis. I use this to open most of my courses and workshops and it is always well received. Delegates find it useful when determining what they want from their training event. (You can learn how to do this on your own training events by turning to Chapter 12.) You can benefit from this great tool as well; here is how it works. It is based on the SWOT tool that marketing departments use when considering launching a new product or service.

In order for this to work effectively, you need to work to a focus statement. You can use the one I have composed here, or compose your own if you feel it would be more appropriate. Draw a square divided into four quadrants, like the one in Table 4.1, then read the focus statement:

> *Focus statement*: Faced with the prospect of becoming a SMART trainer and consistently delivering excellent levels of training delivery and achieving a PEQ™ score rating of 80 per cent plus, candidly write down your current hopes and fears.

From this viewpoint list, in turn, your current strengths, weaknesses, opportunities and threats that you feel would either help or hinder your progress in achieving your goal. Write them down in the appropriate box. Try and be as specific as you can. I will give you a brief overview of each quadrant and how to best tackle it.

Table 4.1 *SWOT analysis*

STRENGTHS	WEAKNESSES
OPPORTUNITIES	THREATS

Strengths

List all of your strengths. What are you good at? In which skill areas do you operate above average most of the time?

It can sometimes be difficult to list many items in this quadrant. One reason is that because we use our skills most of the time we become familiar with the actions and behaviours and we no longer feel they are a skill as such, just something we do. It becomes a habit, so when we analyse it like you are now you don't always recognize it as a skill.

Another reason is a cultural one that affects the British: self-congratulation and positive self-assessment are frowned upon. It's getting better but it still exists. I'll give you a quick example of what I mean.

Tim Henman, the British tennis player, was interviewed during Wimbledon '99 after winning his quarter-final match. In the interview, he said that he believed that his performance was good because he had played with guts. A British newspaper journalist picked up on this and criticized him for being so full of himself, saying that it was up to us (the public/press, etc) to decide whether or not he played with guts.

With that kind of destructive criticism being levelled at us all of the time it is little wonder that we often feel reluctant to peek over the parapet and acknowledge our strengths.

Weaknesses

Weaknesses, on the other hand, seem very easy to pick up on. Please do not be too hard on yourself, but do recognize those skill areas that need further development. It is only by recognizing where you need to focus your self-development energies that you can make quick progress towards your goal of becoming a much sought-after SMART trainer.

Opportunities

The opportunities quadrant will be filled with your list of motivators – what's in it for you by working on yourself. It can be better promotion prospects, higher job satisfaction, increased earnings potential, recognition and acclaim in your field. Make it personal because that's what it is. Visualize the opportunities that can come your way by working on your self-development programme to become a SMART trainer.

Threats

These are the fears we all have. Fears stop us doing the best we can; they stop us achieving what we are really capable of. There is a great book on the market by Dr Susan Jeffers called *Feel the Fear and Do It Anyway*. I strongly recommend this book; I can guarantee it will improve your life and career.

When completing this quadrant think about the things that you perceive could cause you problems. It might be ridicule from people who don't understand your ambitions, or who are envious that you are doing something positive to improve yourself. Again, it's personal, so complete it accordingly.

The threats quadrant is always filled with *perceived* threats and fears. They are not real unless we allow them to become real. So, don't see them as problems or obstacles to your goals, but see them as challenges that you can overcome with the right skill set, knowledge and experience. Keep focused on your objective and the threats will always just be challenges. Remember that obstacles are those scary things we see when we take our eyes off our goal.

YOUR PERSONAL ROUTE TO SMART TRAINER STATUS – FIRST DRAFT

This is the first part of three of your PDP. This framework allows you to pull together all of the key pieces of information about your current training abilities and what you want to achieve in the coming months and years.

Your areas for development must be as accurate as possible, to avoid wasting time and effort and risking disappointment through following the wrong plan. In Table 4.2 write your self-appraisal list, adding comments and suggestions as you go. Remember, it's your own personal and private plan; no one else will see it unless you choose to share it.

All of the following frameworks and structures will be referred back to as you progress through the book. For example, in Chapter 8 you will work on the second draft of your plan with the benefit of the information in Chapters 5, 6 and 7. In Part Three you will do the same. So, get your pen or pencil ready and complete the following as specifically as you can.

The three frameworks to SMART trainer status

The three frameworks that now follow will enable you to focus all your energies in the right direction and on the critical elements. With the help of the previous three chapters and what you have completed in this chapter so far, you can map out your route accurately.

Table 4.2 *Framework 1*

Skill levels, attitudes and behaviours I have identified as being an obstacle to achieving my goal of SMART trainer	*Key recommendations required to initiate improvement in my performance and effectiveness as a trainer*

Once you have completed Table 4.2 as far as you are able move on to the second framework.

Taking stock ready for your PDP blueprint

In each of the boxes within this framework, in Table 4.3, list all the appropriate information you have collected through the previous exercises in this chapter. The information you store here will be useful reference material as you complete the second and final drafts of your PDP.

Table 4.3 *Framework 2*

Current Assets

Strengths	*Key skills used*

Identified Potential

Hidden strengths to develop	*New skills/knowledge required*

Key Changes That Need to Occur

Attitude/behaviours displayed	*Changes recommended*

Complete your first draft

In this third framework, you will have a route plan for your journey to SMART trainer status. In the left-hand box in Table 4.4, write down where you are today in terms of what you feel you are achieving as a trainer, how you're performing, the level of ability and potential you are exercising or displaying.

Table 4.4 *Framework 3*

First Draft Personal Development Plan

Where I am today	What I need to bridge the gap	My one-year desired goal
		My three-year desired goal
		My five-year desired goal

In the right-hand boxes write down where you desire to be, regarding achievements, success, level of performance, skills levels or new skills, behaviours and knowledge.

With both right- and left-hand boxes completed, you can now work on the middle column. This will become your window of opportunity. Establish what you need to acquire, change or become in order to achieve your desired goals. You don't need to go into detail at this stage, a general idea will be sufficient as you will discover new things about yourself and come across a whole host of different ideas as you work your way through the next two parts of the book. This first draft will form the important foundation for you to place the building blocks of your PDP.

Carry out a mindstorming session and place as many thoughts and ideas as you can in the boxes over a 15- to 20-minute period. It doesn't matter if you later change your mind or discover something better; that's what first drafts are all about.

Think in ink

Write down any key issues you wish to explore in the next part of this book. You could also write down any questions you would like to ask, and e-mail my free 'Questions and answers for SMART trainers' service, on kencoach@aol.com.

The SMART trainer's summary of Chapter 4

In summary, you covered, learnt and worked on the following key factors that will help you achieve Beyond Traditional Training status by investing in your own development and becoming a SMART trainer:

- your starting point – where you are now;
- list of SMART questions;
- self-assessment inventory;
- four stages of learning;
- PEQ™;
- personal SWOT analysis;
- first draft of your PDP.

PART TWO

LOOK, LISTEN AND LEARN

This section will arm you with enough information to complete the second draft of your Personal Development Plan (PDP). It will also share with you and explain how to put into practice a number of the critical skills, strategies and techniques that SMART trainers use. In order to do this as effectively as possible you will witness training in action.

ROLE MODELS FOR MODEL ROLES

Most trainers operate in the TRADITIONAL trainer mode for most of the time. You may believe that you operate as anything but a TRADITIONAL type of trainer. I ask you to briefly suspend judgement and check out your performance through the following three important chapters.

Through this part of the book you will be introduced to a variety of training role models. Not all of them will be pleasant or good to follow. By looking at the bad, the indifferent and the SMART, you will discover the crucial next steps on your PDP.

Three of the next four chapters will display to you key behaviours and attitudes that all have an impact on the delegates in the training room and the clients' bottom line. There will obviously be more minor behaviours that make up each of these trainer types, but during these sessions we will concentrate on the major ones. Some of these training demonstrations you will recognize first-hand, often in others and sometimes in yourself. Don't worry too much. The evidence put before you is not designed to convict you of a crime against innocent learners of the corporate world. See it as a means to an end.

You can only change your style, behaviours and thinking habits from negative or TRADITIONALIST methods to positive and productive ones once you can fully recognize what they look, sound and feel like. See this part of the book as a process designed to act as a series of building blocks that will enable you to successfully add to the Stage 3 of learning.

FINE-TUNING YOUR DEVELOPMENT

This part of the book is crucial in the fine-tuning of your Action Plan. Here you will be able to build further on the steps you placed on your first draft in Chapter 4.

You will see just what a NIGHTMARE trainer looks, sounds and behaves like. I will warn you here, it is not a pretty sight.

You will discover the key flaws of TRADITIONAL trainers. They are, generally, good people with the best of intentions. However, it's worth reminding ourselves here that the road to hell is paved with good intentions. There will be some actions that TRADITIONAL trainers should be encouraged to keep doing, but there are many that they need encouraging to stop doing. Many of the behaviours that TRADITIONAL trainers fail to demonstrate are often due to lack of confidence and self-belief, so they are easy to change and put right.

While you work your way through Chapters 5 and 6 you will be shown alternative behaviours, attitudes and strategies that if put into practice would remove the negative traits from your current performance.

You will also learn the crucial habits and strategies of the SMART trainer as you observe them in full action. This will be achieved through various case studies and other observations where you will discover how a TRADITIONAL or NIGHTMARE trainer behaved. This experience will then explore what the SMART trainer would have done in the same circumstances. You will then be able to clearly determine the differences between the three key training styles. You will also be able to pick out the elements of each one that are currently part of your style. It will prepare you well for the next part of your Action Plan for SMART training status.

All of the scenarios that you will witness over the next few chapters are true experiences, only the names and places have been changed to protect the innocent and the fragile egos of the arrogant and guilty. Read on, learn and enjoy.

The four chapters in this part are:

5. The NIGHTMARE trainer observed;
6. The TRADITIONAL trainer observed;
7. The SMART trainer observed;
8. Building on the foundations of your action plan – Action Plan Part II.

This part of the book is equivalent to day two of the Master Class workshop.

Prepare yourself for you may discover some of your own sins as you work your way through this session. It will also confirm any 'best practice' activities that you have been implementing in your own courses. This session will prepare you well for your next Action Plan draft.

5

THE NIGHTMARE TRAINER OBSERVED

'The goal of effective communication should be for the listener to say, "Me too!" versus "So what?"'

(Jim Rohn)

> **Your learning objectives in this chapter**
>
> By studying the examples, recorded experiences and real-life case studies in this chapter you will be able to:
>
> - recognize the critical behaviours and attitudes of NIGHTMARE trainers that plague and turn off their delegates;
> - evaluate your own current training impact on your delegates by comparing the NIGHTMARE trainer behaviour traits with your own;
> - prepare yourself for the next steps for a clear strategy to avoid NIGHTMARE trainer pitfalls and to train yourself out of NIGHTMARE trainer habits.

SETTING THE SCENE

Whenever I carry out a review and feedback session I always start with the negative and move on to the positive. This part of the book will get that same treatment. We will start with the trainer who likes to have absolute control and power, usually at any cost to the delegates' wellbeing. The key to the NIGHTMARE trainers' problem is communication, or their communication style, and the fact that they consistently make assumptions about their delegates' needs and wants. They often see their delegates as people inferior to themselves and we know what happens to our behaviour towards people if we believe something to be true about them. Let's explore this here.

WHAT'S IN A NAME?

NIGHTMARE really is an appropriate name for this type of trainer, although I do acknowledge that there are a number of variations on the theme. In fact you will find that there are a number of NIGHTMARE levels on which this type of trainer usually operates. The purpose of this chapter though, is to recognize the key character traits and behaviours and, just as importantly, to see if you can recognize any of those traits in your own training style.

What if you do recognize any of the NIGHTMARE behaviours in yourself? Well, as I've said before, don't be too hard on yourself. After all, what's gone before is now history and no one can do anything to change that. What's done is done. And even SMART trainers have done some NIGHTMARE things in the past, while they were developing their SMART skills. I know I did in the very early days of my career.

The best advice I can give you is to be totally honest with yourself. If you do recognize any behaviours that you have acted out in the training room in the past then put your hand up to them. Acknowledge that there is a better, more productive way of doing it, and vow to adopt the better way in the future. All trainers are only as good as the next training course or workshop that they deliver. Remember, nobody was born a SMART trainer; they all had to learn their craft.

IT'S ALL IN THE FOCUS

The key element that separates the NIGHTMARE trainer from the SMART trainer is that of focus. Inward focus is the main criteria for the NIGHTMARE trainer. All of their training events, even basic presentations, are trainer driven and trainer led. All or most of their energies are targeted towards themselves, how they're feeling, what they want, what's in it for them.

When asked, they tell you a good story of how much the delegates' welfare means to them. This can be very easily revealed as pure lip-service through their actions during the training event. One of their major problems is that they make sweeping assumptions about their audiences, particularly about their levels of intellect and intelligence.

THE BAD GUYS OF TRAINING

If these trainers were cowboys (and in a way they are!) they would be wearing black hats. I make no bones about the fact that I want to drive these trainers out of the profession, not them personally you understand, just their behaviours and attitudes. Obviously, if they are not prepared to recognize how destructive their methods are for everyone, and change them, then they must be changed for better trainers – replaced with SMART trainers.

At this point I must put things into a clearer perspective. NIGHTMARE trainers are relatively rare among the total number of trainers. There can appear to be more of them than there really are because of the far-reaching damage they cause. If you are familiar with distribution curves then you will recognize Figure 5.1. You can put NIGHTMARE trainers and SMART trainers at the opposite extremes of a trainer style/impact continuum. The middle ground is where all the TRADITIONAL trainers reside.

As you can see, the vast majority of trainers will fall into the centre ground category of TRADITIONAL trainer. So, you may find that only a few NIGHTMARE trainer traits will apply. There are very few out-and-out NIGHTMARE trainers, thank goodness.

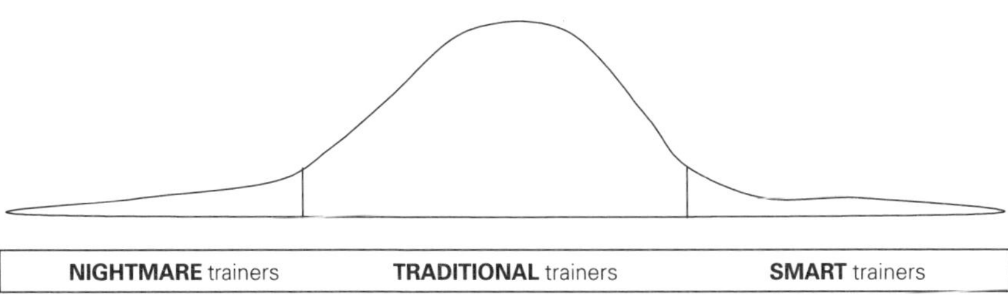

Figure 5.1 *Trainer style/impact distribution curve*

Don't settle for average

TRADITIONAL trainers make up the vast majority, which means that all those who fall into this category work in the middle ground. They work, as a general rule, to an average performance standard. Although average may not be bad, it can't be described as being that good either. This is because, in reality, it isn't good it's, well, just average. I want you to become better than average, consistently performing at a higher level than average. Achieving peak performance, which is consistently hitting your personal best, must become your aim.

I want you to go beyond average, and therefore beyond TRADITIONAL. SMART trainers never settle for second best; after all, that's what average really is – second best. We'll deal with the TRADITIONAL trainer traits in the next chapter; for now let's get back to NIGHTMARE trainers and explore just what they are responsible for. We'll start with some examples.

There are two aspects of the NIGHTMARE trainer, which reside at extremes to each other: one is feelings of superiority, the other feelings of inferiority. Both are negative experiences from the point of view of the delegate and both are preventable. We'll look at both of these behaviour types in turn.

THE NIGHTMARE TRAINER IN ACTION – PART 1

First, let's look at the egotistical specimen. This trainer exudes confidence and an air of superiority. If one phrase could best sum up this type of NIGHTMARE trainer it would have to be 'know-it-all'. This type of NIGHTMARE trainer truly believes that he or she is superior to the audience in every way. And it shows.

Do you recognize anyone yet? I'll give you some more examples. This type of NIGHTMARE trainer communicates in a patronizing style, often ploughing on with his or her training inputs without a worry in the world and, more critically, without an ounce of consideration for the audience.

They often deliver turgid masses of information on their given subject with very little audience participation. Or, having read somewhere that activities on training courses help with the learning process, intersperse their input sessions with a little game or two. The delegates play out these games, but they always fall well short of being of any real use. The NIGHTMARE trainer usually fails to draw any parallels with the workplace, and the training activity remains as just a trivial game used to break up the input session.

To communicate or to connect

The communication process is very simple for NIGHTMARE trainers: they see it as something they do to others. If delegates don't connect with the NIGHTMARE trainer's communication style then it's always the delegate's fault. They train *at* the delegate not *with* them. And this loops us back to focus. The NIGHTMARE trainer is inward focused.

The NIGHTMARE trainer hasn't realized just how complex the communication process of humans really is. The words we use, the tone of voice used in speaking them and the body language we adopt as we speak, are very important but only the tip of the communication iceberg.

The other dimensions

All SMART trainers know that the secret ingredient to winning over an audience and taking them with you every step of the way is rapport. Unfortunately, the NIGHTMARE trainer hasn't learnt how to create this magical component of the language. Remember, they are know-it-alls; they don't need to learn any new stuff. After all they are far too busy teaching it to the ignorant masses.

They are also blissfully unaware of the powers of NLP (neuro-linguistic programming).[1] Sure they may have heard of it, but they either poo-poo it as US psychobabble or suffer from the self-delusion of knowing all about it from scanning one article on the subject in a magazine.

My wife, Jeannette, who is a partner in our Peak Performance consultancy and runs our telephone coaching department, came across a NIGHTMARE trainer while attending a training course herself. This training consultant, attending the same course, initially gave a good impression, for about 30 minutes. She then became an overbearing bore about how brilliant she was at everything in the training field. She claimed that she was an expert on NLP but proceeded to get every assessment of other people's preferred communication style incorrect.

This, however, did not faze or deter her. And this insensitivity to others and lack of awareness are really what makes a potentially SMART trainer into a NIGHTMARE trainer instead.

Interestingly, her attendance at the training course may have indicated to the uninitiated that she was dedicated to personal improvement; sadly, the reality behind her behaviours gave her away. Here's why.

The course, on achieving peak performance, was over three days. She decided to turn up an hour after the course had started on day two. She took no notes of her own, but on noticing Jeannette taking down key strategies and information, asked her to send a copy on to her. Her attention kept wandering and she kept whispering to people sat near her. During the breaks, when she spoke with others, her listening skills were conspicuous by their absence. She left the course, on some pretext, straight after lunch. She never returned for day three.

Interestingly we saw an advert this 'training consultant' had placed in a professional publication that literally screamed, 'Look at me, ain't I great.' Which left you feeling cold and saying, 'So what!'

What I'd give to be a fly on the wall in one of her training sessions. I don't think that she is a lost cause though, not if she can open her mind to real personal development and raise her awareness of how her current behaviour is affecting others in such a negative way.

Attitudes breed behaviours

NIGHTMARE trainers have an attitude problem. They look at the training event as something that has to be delivered *at* the audience. They have a set of sessions that they have prepared, and that is what they are going to deliver, come what may.

Deviation is not in the vocabulary of the 'superior' NIGHTMARE trainer. If the delegates would benefit from a slight shift in emphasis on the training material, then why are they on this course?

This type of NIGHTMARE trainer has neither the skills nor the inclination to move away from his or her planned programme, and that is usually because the programme was planned from the trainer's viewpoint and not, as it always should be, the delegates' real needs.

They also have very low skills in the art of listening actively and being able to read body language. And again, this is all down to focus. If you are constantly looking inward you will always miss the telltale signs that your delegates send your way. You will pick up on these if things are going wrong, and be able to adjust your training input accordingly, but remember, you will also be able to gain valuable feedback when your training is going well and hitting its target.

THE NIGHTMARE TRAINER IN ACTION – PART 2 – THE TRADE DESCRIPTIONS ACT!

There are trainers out there, and no doubt you have come across one or two yourself, or know someone who has, who would be prosecuted under the Trade Descriptions Act if it were possible. They claim to be trainers and then behave in a way that defies that very description. Let me share with you another true example, presented to me by a good friend who was sent on a course in the line of his new job. Admittedly the subject matter was potentially as dry as old toast. However, in the league of SMART trainers that is no excuse. My friend, John, had to attend a one-day course on contract law and the trainer did the following: no training. That's right, he did no training yet the event was advertised as a training course, and the person running it was billed as the trainer. This is what actually took place.

John turned up for the training course in time for registration and coffee. The course started promptly at 9 am. The trainer sat at the front of the room, behind a desk with his pipe in his hand. Yes, you did read correctly, a pipe. He smoked this on and off for the duration. Already this has the hallmarks of a travesty of training, but it gets worse.

The trainer had a manual open in front of him and it was from this that every piece of information about contract law was read. It was read from 9 am through to 11 am when, much to everyone's relief, a 20-minute coffee break allowed them some respite.

They were all back being read to from 11.20 am through to 1 pm when there was a one-hour lunch break. The afternoon consisted of two sessions running from 2 pm through to 3.30 pm and then 3.50 pm through to 5 pm.

There were no introductions at the beginning of the day, there were no activities, no questioning of the delegates at any stage throughout the day and no encouragement of the delegates to ask questions.

My friend John told me that it was the most depressingly boring day he had ever experienced in his life. And what made it all the worse for John was that the trainer seemed totally oblivious to the effect he was having on his delegates. He didn't even talk with anyone during the breaks.

I asked John what he felt he had learnt from this so-called 'training' event. He thought for a moment and then said that it had taught him to avoid training courses like the plague in future. He also confirmed what I already knew would have taken place very early on in the day: that within half an hour of the course starting he had tuned out. As had everyone else in the room. What a pitiful waste of everybody's time and money. It's a crime.

Change or be changed

In my opinion trainers like the one we've just experienced through my friend John, should be encouraged to change, or failing that, changed for a better trainer. I mean, we don't allow surgeons to continue to operate on people's bodies once we've discovered that they are incompetent. Trainers are no different, except that they operate on people's minds.

Training is about transferring knowledge, skills and techniques to others so that they may work more effectively and efficiently. John's trainer transferred absolutely nothing of value. The only thing he transferred successfully was that training courses are a waste of time, effort and money. SMART trainers could do without this hurdle to get their delegates over before beginning their own courses.

So, you can see what I mean about the Trade Descriptions Act: the guy was not really a trainer, but someone masquerading as one. His biggest sins were not giving a damn about the delegates in his charge, and failing to get over important knowledge and skills that the delegates needed in order to do their jobs competently. Strike him off!

THE NIGHTMARE TRAINER IN ACTION – PART 3

Besides the NIGHTMARE trainer with the superiority complex there is also the specimen at the other end of the trainer continuum. This trainer suffers from an inferiority complex and has a self-confidence problem. These trainers try so hard to be liked and accepted by the group that they succeed in doing the exact opposite.

They also are guilty of making assumptions about their audiences. It will depend on the subject they are training. For example, while the arrogant NIGHTMARE trainers assume their audiences are not bright enough to understand certain subjects, passive NIGHTMARE trainers will assume they will become bored.

Here's an example. I sat in on a trainer's workshop about 18 months ago in order to get a feel for the course. This was to help me to decide whether or not I wanted to run the same course for a training company that wanted me to carry out some associate work. This happens quite a lot these days as more and more training organizations approach me to run programmes for them. This has helped me with the development of my Train-the-Trainer Master Class workshops and my own development, as there is much to learn from other trainers, both good and bad. And, of course, it has helped me immensely with the material for this book. The course structure and content was good, but the trainer....

The trainer had a great deal of experience in the role of stand-up training, yet he still didn't really enjoy it. You always felt that he wanted to get it over with so that he could go back home to safety.

While I observed the way the course ran I also assessed the trainer. I could see that he had the potential to become a SMART trainer. However, he would lapse, at regular intervals, into NIGHTMARE trainer traits, and with disastrous effects on his audience.

The power of auto-suggestion

I also call this the power of the self-fulfilling prophecy. The best place to see this happening in front of your very eyes is on the golf course. You don't like golf. It doesn't matter, just go along for the fun of observing people enjoying themselves in a masochistic sort of way.

All golf high handicappers suffer from the same problem. They underestimate how powerful a role the mind plays in the game. The high handicappers will tee up their shot and look towards the fairway, scanning the scene for information that will help them plan their shot. On seeing a bunker a hundred yards to the left of the fairway their confidence takes an immediate hit. They then start repeating over and over in their mind, 'I bet it goes in the bunker, I hate bunkers, I always go in the bunker, I bet it goes in the bunker.'

Now those of us who now how the mind works could tell those golfers that whatever they are focusing on, in this case the bunker, is where they are going to be aiming. So, once the ball is hit its landing place will rarely disappoint: it will land in or very near that dreaded bunker. The self-fulfilling prophecy comes true. They then compound the problem they have beset themselves with by saying, almost triumphantly, 'There, I told you.'

As there are only two types of self-fulfilling prophecy it shouldn't be difficult to choose the right one, especially as one of the choices is negative and the other is positive.

So, back to my observed trainer and his auto-suggestion trick. He was delivering a programme that consisted of a fair amount of statistics and calculations. The workshop was designed to run with teams of four to six people per team so they could work together for support; it also made it more fun, especially as some of the teamwork was competitive.

Right from the outset of the day the trainer came over as apologetic. It would probably be better if I gave you a blow-by-blow account of his NIGHTMARE trainer errors. Here is a brief rundown of what happened as the day unfolded.

He said, 'Good morning!' and then it went down hill. Our observed trainer was a nice enough guy, but nice enough guys do not make effective trainers if they aren't performing in the appropriate way. Organizations pay good money for the training of their staff and they want it to have an impact on their people's behaviour, productivity and bottom line.

Our trainer spent very little time on the introductions. For the SMART trainer introductions are a crucial step in the building of trainer and audience rapport.[2] Our trainer did nothing to build his credibility. This is also a major error of many TRADITIONAL trainers. Believe me, if you do not establish your credibility with your delegates you will never fully carry them with you for the duration of the training programme.

He also failed to ask the crucial question during the introductions, that question being: 'What do you want to gain from attending this workshop?' This meant that he lost a major opportunity to get his delegates to buy into the day's events.

From the very brief introductions he went straight into the objectives of the day. And then... and then he began to apologize. He apologized for the course they were on because it meant that they would have to do a few 'boring' things. It was at this point that I did a double-take. Did I hear correctly? Did he actually say that they would be trained in a few boring things? Yes he did. Unfortunately things never improved.

Repetition is the mother of skill… and believing a message. Throughout the training day this trainer repeated the phrase, 'I know that you will find this next part boring, because it's working with boring figures, but it has to be done.' Or, 'I'm sorry for this next bit, it's going to be a bit boring.'

He always looked like he was at odds with his audience. His energy levels during his delivery session left a lot to be desired. And his audience looked – yes, you've guessed correctly – bored. In fact, because of his habit of repeating a whole host of negative phrases along with his 'boring' one, he created a powerful self-fulfilling prophecy.

Proof of the self-fulfilling prophecy

This particular trainer was one of two who delivered these workshops and a few weeks later I was fortunate to be sat in on the other trainer for the day. What a contrast.

This other trainer was a SMART trainer. And how it showed. He didn't skimp on the introductions, he got people involved early on and sold himself with the appropriate anecdotes and examples in order to establish his credibility as quickly as possible. His energy levels were well balanced. He didn't apologize once. He made it fun. And his audience enjoyed it and learnt what they were there to learn.

Mr Boring plodded on through the day talking in terms that nobody could relate to. And by the afternoon, nobody wanted to anyway. Their interest levels were in the minus figures; their minds were most definitely somewhere else.

Mr Fun took them on a magical mystery tour. They came expecting the worst but found something much better, to their complete surprise. Their feedback sheets reflected their experience.

The clues are in the feedback

During the lunch break on Mr Fun's workshop a delegate said to me in passing that he was dreading this course. When I pressed him for a reason he said it was because he had heard from his colleagues who had attended earlier workshops that it was really boring. Now I wonder how that could have happened?

A good test that tells you whether you are delivering your subject well, that you are delivering it in the SMART trainer mode, is when a delegate speaks to you in glowing terms during the course or at the end of the day.

I have witnessed this in other trainers' courses I have been attending and have experienced it myself on numerous occasions, when a delegate approaches you and says, 'I didn't want to come on this course, but you know, I'm really glad I did. I've learnt so much and it's been enjoyable.' It's difficult to put into words just how good that makes the trainer feel. When you win over the reluctant attendee then you know you are working well for the good of your delegates.

MY FAMILY AND OTHER ANIMALS

I eat, live and breathe training and the positive impact it can have on people's lives, so I see the training profession as a family. And it's very enjoyable when you meet other like-minded people who have had similar experiences who you can readily relate to.

Then there are the other animals masquerading as family – the NIGHTMARE trainers. Whether it is through their misguided beliefs or just plain ignorance, the damage that they can inflict on innocent delegates through their attitudes and behaviours is criminal.

This type of trainer causes problems for all of us real 'professionals'. It causes problems that the SMART trainer can see only too well. I come across such damage on most courses I run. I train, on average, 800 people every year and most could relate to me a bad training experience they have endured at some time in their working life.

It also causes problems for the TRADITIONAL trainer too, only most of them are blissfully ignorant of the fact. This is due to their awareness levels operating below par. Just by raising your awareness on a number of simple levels you can lift your performance up a few notches.[3]

You may be thinking that I'm over-reacting by referring to NIGHTMARE trainers as animals, but you must remember I have travelled many times in the wake of their damaging style. I have seen the pain they have caused their delegates. That is not what they are paid good money to do. They must be changed or chased off.

The damage these trainers cause, which other trainers following them have to deal with, is unnecessary and preventable. However, until we can eliminate all NIGHTMARE trainers we are going to have to deal with each situation as it arises. You will be taken through tried and tested strategies of dealing with NIGHTMARE trainer damage in Chapter 12, which, as I have indicated before, you can jump forward to if you so wish.

Examples of NIGHTMARE trainer damage

I have encountered so many examples over my 15 plus years in up-front training that to list them all would become tedious and very long-winded. Many of the examples are similar anyway, although to the delegate they are unique, so I have decided to share with you a few of the more serious ones.

Recently I had to run a one-day follow-up workshop where a different trainer ran the original two-day workshop. Once I had secured the delegates' confidence and relaxed them so that they could gain the maximum benefit from their learning experience, one delegate expressed her unhappiness over the original two-day course.

She told me how the trainer had consistently undermined her self-confidence because he always criticized her inputs, whether it was offering a suggestion, answering a question, or taking part in a role-play. She said that she was very reluctant to attend the follow-up day. I could see why.

Feedback from other delegates on the same trainer confirmed this behaviour and added other elements, such as arrogance, mild bullying and lack of audience buy-in. I had to ensure that the balance was redressed before I could successfully transfer the new skills and knowledge.

The most damaging aspect is when a delegate is attending their first training course since starting work. Their last learning experience is school, and most people have rather negative experiences of school stored away in their subconscious. If people are exposed to a NIGHTMARE trainer on their first ever training course then that is their perception of adult learning. And they will do almost anything to avoid having to repeat it. Can you blame them?

I have come across incidences where trainers obviously delight in humiliating and embarrassing their delegates, insisting that they come up to the front of the group and role-play even when it's obvious they're petrified. Why do trainers do that? The delegate receives no benefit from it at all.

Presentation skills courses often bring out the sadistic side of many NIGHTMARE trainers. One incident was related to me by a training administrator I was meeting to discuss course dates for an upcoming programme. She told me that towards the end of the first day of a presentation skills course she had to go into the room to hand the trainer some photocopying that he requested. She noticed that one of the delegates (a man) was crying. She assumed that he had received some bad news. A few minutes after leaving the training room the trainer popped into her office to borrow a hole-punch. She asked him if everything was all right. He looked at her a little puzzled. She told him that she had noticed one of the delegates crying. He became quite dismissive, saying that he always used the method of breaking them down first before building them up. He was quite proud of these draconian measures. The training administrator was appalled. Thankfully he was never asked back so at least her people were spared the nightmare.

The clear up

On a few occasions I have been called in to a company to repair the damage caused by a rogue trainer, or a trainer operating out of his or her depth. I have to admit that while I am not pleased at the evidence of some quite appalling training practices, it is highly satisfying getting people to experience the good side of training.

One such occasion was to do with train-the-trainer courses. The company concerned wanted about 120 shop floor operatives trained as on-job trainers, so that they could cover all aspects of that type of training: new starters, multi-skilling, etc. The first two groups (there were 12 groups of 10 over three months) were quite hostile to this training. I had to discover the cause of this hostility as quickly as possible if the whole programme was to be a success.

On doing some focused questioning, most of it during the breaks, I discovered that they had been put on a similar programme 18 months ago. However, the consultant had misunderstood the brief and he had delivered a presentation skills course. They were put through a series of training sessions that taught them how to deliver a training session as a presentation to a group in a classroom. This was never going to happen in the work place. He also used methods that were completely unrelated to their working environment, like getting them to lie on the floor and resist other delegates trying to pick them up. Of course they switched off.

Besides misunderstanding the original brief, or just as bad, failing to fully clarify the exact requirements and expectations of the client, this trainer had also failed to take notice of or act on the very clear signals the delegates were obviously sending him as he attempted to train them.

KEY BEHAVIOUR TRAITS OF THE NIGHTMARE TRAINER

I think you've had enough examples of this particular beast and no doubt could add some of your own. Let's look at the key behaviour traits of this type of trainer, shown in Table 5.1, and then move on to the next chapter, which will deal with TRADITIONAL trainers and their behaviours and attitudes that cause concern.

Table 5.1 *Key behaviour traits of aggressive and passive NIGHTMARE trainers*

Aggressive **NIGHTMARE** trainer	Passive **NIGHTMARE** trainer
■ Over confident	■ Lacks confidence
■ Treats assumptions as facts	■ Treats assumptions as facts
■ Arrogant	■ Lacks self belief
■ Inflexible	■ Inferiority complex
■ Superiority complex	■ Indecisive
■ Know it all	■ Allows events to control him or her
■ Dismissive of others' suggestions if they clash with his or her own	■ Uncomfortable
■ Bullying	■ Uses negative phrasing
■ Patronizing	■ Undersells self
■ Condescending	

The SMART trainer's summary of Chapter 5

In summary, you covered, learnt and worked on the following key factors that will help you achieve Beyond Traditional Training status by investing in your own development and becoming a SMART trainer:

- what is meant by NIGHTMARE trainer;
- the two main types of NIGHTMARE trainer;
- the focus of the NIGHTMARE trainer;
- the trainer type distribution curve;
- NIGHTMARE trainers in action;
- the power of auto-suggestion;
- examples of NIGHTMARE trainer damage;
- key behaviour traits of the two main types of NIGHTMARE trainer.

Notes

1. More on this is Chapters 11 and 12.
2. Key tips and tricks of the trade are covered in Chapter 11.
3. You will discover how in Chapter 9.

6

THE TRADITIONAL TRAINER OBSERVED

'If someone is going down the wrong road, they don't need motivation to speed them up. What they need is education to turn them round.'

(Jim Rohn)

Your learning objectives in this chapter

By studying the examples, recorded experiences and real-life case studies in this chapter you will be able to:

- recognize the critical behaviours and attitudes that hinder the delegates of TRADITIONAL trainers;
- evaluate your current training impact on your delegates by assessing your own training style and skills against those of the TRADITIONAL trainer;
- develop the next steps for a clear strategy to avoid TRADITIONAL trainer pitfalls.

THE PURPOSE AND SCOPE OF THIS CHAPTER

This session of the Train-the-Trainer Master Class programme allows the delegates to explore the key attitudes and behaviours of a typical TRADITIONAL trainer. It is important to recognize whether any of these attitudes and behaviours are being displayed or demonstrated through your training preparation and delivery.

Through this chapter you will make some great discoveries of how not to do it, and that some of those bad habits, incorrect or outdated methods will be part of your current style of delivery. You may also find that you are already applying some of the SMART trainer ways of delivering theory or other elements of training but didn't realize it, so you will have certain aspects confirmed for you.

If you do discover that you have some TRADITIONAL trainer traits, and more than likely you will, don't worry about it. They are just habits and like all habits, whether mental or physical, they can be broken and replaced with positive alternatives. So, let's have a look at this most common type of training style.

SAFE AND COMFORTABLE

TRADITIONAL trainers like to feel safe and comfortable. They also suffer from some of the NIGHTMARE trainer traits but in a milder form. Their minds tend to be a little on the closed side; they avoid anything too radical or adventurous. I suppose a good term for many of these trainers would be 'blinkered'.

Their world is one of time schedules and routines, rules and regulations, rights and wrongs, good and bad. They keep to the well-established methods no matter how long ago they may have been superseded. Updated methods, in general, are not to be encouraged. All in all TRADITIONAL trainers like the thoroughly tried if not altogether fully tested methods of training delivery. They believe, however, that these methods *are* fully tested due to the fact that they have been using the same methods for many years and have grown so accustomed to them. To them they are tested, but we know that this is in theory only. And theory is very important to the TRADITIONAL trainer.

Theory is the mental bindweed of training courses

To TRADITIONAL trainers theory is what really matters. They have brains stuffed full of theories, concepts and models. Now don't get me wrong, this is not the part that I'm critical of. SMART trainers also use theories, concepts and models and they firmly believe that there is always a place for them in their trainer's armoury. However, it is the teaching of the practical application of those theories and concepts that is so often missing or lacking in the TRADITIONAL trainer's delivery. This hampers the delegates on their return to work in putting what they have learnt to any real and profitable use.

I am not saying that you have to cut out the theory in your training. That is totally unrealistic. In any subject that you teach, an element of theory is required before some practice can take place. What you need is to be aware of the best way to deliver the theory of any topic. When preparing your training course material you should be asking yourself the following SMART trainer questions:

- How much of the theory should I be looking to deliver in any one go?
- In what style or styles would it best be delivered?
- How can I best deliver it with a little bit of pizzazz?
- What time of the day is the best for my delegates to take in and assimilate the information?
- Do I know what the SMART trainer way is?

There is the TRADITIONAL way to deliver it and the SMART trainer way of delivering it. If you are still stuck in TRADITIONAL trainer ways then you will not know the answer to the last question.

Let's develop this 'theory' delivery debate a little further. A training cliché that everyone is familiar with is the following.

The 'talk and chalk' syndrome

Have you ever experienced a lecture? Now, if the lecturer was someone with charisma and massive amounts of passion for the subject then, and only then, could he or she hold your attention for any period of time.

Think back to your university days. Did all the lectures you attended hold you spell bound for their whole duration? Or did the 60-minute talk feel like 60 days? I bet I know the answer.

One of the main pitfalls that TRADITIONAL trainers fall into is the 'chalk and talk' syndrome. There are a number of reasons for this, which we will now explore together. If you recognize any in your own delivery style then make sure you make a note of them for later inclusion in your SMART trainer blueprint.

Your 'talk and chalk' style is a habit. It's what you've always done. You were trained to train this way. We know that most TRADITIONAL trainers were either self-taught, and therefore muddled their way through by trial and error, or were trained by well-established TRADITIONAL trainers who mistakenly believed they were SMART trainers.

What does 'talk and chalk' really mean? Whenever I hear this phrase I always picture a trainer stood at the front of the training room, almost glued to the side of a flipchart, marker pen in hand, poised for action, talking at the audience.

The 'talk and chalk' merchants don't permit the audience to become too involved with the session. If the trainer asks any questions they are usually rhetorical ones. They don't demand anything of their audience, just that they sit there and at least look like they're listening. Now, maybe some are listening, but I can guarantee that most won't be. Let's be honest, would you enjoy training sessions, one after the other, where you are incessantly talked at?

Audiences crave involvement. They want to get in on the action, they want the opportunity to show off some of their knowledge, they want to feel valued, and they want to learn and improve. They hate being bored. Which means that they hate being sat stock-still looking at you statically rambling on. Oh, yes, there is no doubt that you have real nuggets of wisdom to share, but that isn't enough for the vast majority of people. They want to be entertained while they're being trained.

When I say that your audience, and I mean every audience, wants to be entertained, I don't mean with jokes and slapstick routines. Entertainment comes in many guises; the best three are easily delivered in the training room. And they are involvement, involvement, and involvement:

- involvement during the input sessions through questioning and challenging;
- involvement through working on case studies;
- involvement through working in teams on activities or simulations.

Being involved in something practical will drive home the key learning points in a way that makes them stick in the memory long enough for them to be useful once the delegates get back to the workplace.

Never forget you are there to get your delegates to transfer their new skills and knowledge to their real jobs on return from your course. This is the overall purpose of your job and is critical for the good of the training profession.

There are a number of options open to the trainer in achieving delegate involvement that enables the learning process to move up to top gear. A good sign to look out for that tells you whether you are delivering your subject in the TRADITIONAL trainer or SMART trainer mode is the delegates' reaction to major break times.

Whenever a SMART trainer gets to the lunch break, or more often at the end of the first day of a two-day course, at least one delegate will mention that they didn't realize that was the time, or say, 'Today went quickly'. Do delegates ever say that on your courses? If so, well done, keep it up. If not, don't worry, they soon will.

There is never any excuse for 'talk and chalk' sessions in their purest form. Sure some sessions of information input are needed and that is why SMART trainers have a method that creates audience involvement. They also operate to a golden rule of timing, which you will discover and learn how to put into practice immediately. Let's have a look at some of the reasons behind the TRADITIONAL trainer's love of the 'talk and chalk' method.

A lack of confidence through loss of control

In many cases it is a lack of confidence in their ability to deal with audience inputs that ties trainers to the 'talk and chalk' method. What if a delegate asks a question that hadn't been anticipated? Or, it could be a lack of confidence in their ability to keep the course on track. Many people feel safer when they are in control of all of the events. In most cases it is both of these elements that trigger the TRADITIONAL trainer behaviour. The problem is compounded by the fact that by keeping on the 'talk and chalk' track you effectively strangle the life out of the group of people you are training. SMART trainers fully understand and know how to manipulate[1] group dynamics.

When running the Train-the-Trainer Master Class we work hard with the participants to help them overcome this very common obstacle to achieving SMART trainer status. They always come through, because it isn't really that difficult to deal with once you do three things:

1. You recognize that this is one of your traits.
2. You recognize that there are many ways of eliminating the cause of the problem.
3. You commit yourself to putting the SMART trainer techniques into practice.

Time – the trainer's friend or enemy?

With delivering training the critical factor is time. You never have enough of it. At least you don't if you allow any audience involvement. Start asking delegates questions, or even more adventurous, allowing delegates to ask you questions, eats up masses of those precious minutes that you use as the building blocks of your timetable.

Whenever you hand over a training session to your delegates, through an activity or case study, you effectively hand them control of time for that period. They will always need longer to complete the activity and will always take longer to get to and from the break-out room.[2] And it is this factor, more than any other, that tempts the TRADITIONAL trainer down the path of 'talk and chalk' training.

You promised the client what?

There is an easy way to tell if a person who has a TRADITIONAL trainer mindset has organized the training with a client. Now a client here could mean many things. If you are an employed trainer then it would be the line managers you have to deal with, or your boss. If you are an independent consultant then it would obviously be your paying customers. I will give you an example from my experiences with some blue chip companies as both employed training officer and manager and as an independent training consultant.

As an independent consultant who works as an associate for various training companies I am very rarely the person who goes in and sells the training event. A sales account manager, who has relevant knowledge and experience of training courses and programmes, deals directly with the client and their perceived needs. Whenever I am assigned a project to work on I am sent a copy of the training programme proposal so that I can prepare the training event appropriately. Somctimes it's a one-day workshop, sometimes it's two days.

Whatever the duration of the programme that has been agreed I always find myself exclaiming, 'They want all of this in one day!' There will be 10 or more objectives and up to 20 areas of differing content. All good stuff, but to train people to actually be able to put all of it into practice within one day – I don't think so.

Of course the TRADITIONAL trainer will not have the same problem as all of their sessions will be based on 'talk and chalk'. So a series of interlinking lectures will cover the content of the programme.

No matter that the audience will have switched off after just one session and have been sat there in body only.

The SMART trainer has to learn how to prioritize and then focus on the critical skills that will enable the delegates to go back to their jobs and begin making a more positive difference. Of course the SMART trainer also knows that this is a two-part process. The first part is carried out by the trainer during the preparation stage and the second part during the opening sessions with the delegates, because they must buy into the day's events.

You will discover just what takes place when you get to the next chapter, 'The SMART trainer observed', and learn exactly how to master the key strategies in order to raise your performance to SMART trainer status in Part Three. In the meantime we'll move on to the next problem area that the TRADITIONAL trainers create for themselves.

BUT I DO COMMUNICATE – DON'T I?

The other negative factor about the 'talk and chalk' method is the block it creates with building rapport. Let's look at some typical problems that delegates face when rapport-building is hindered.

The problem with communication is that most of us believe that we are really good at it simply because it is something that we have been doing for years. Well, since we were born really. It seems so easy: you talk, I listen; then I talk and you listen. Now we already know from an earlier chapter that there is a major discrepancy between the speed at which we talk and the speed at which we think to ourselves. There are also other areas of conflict that we need to understand and know how to counter.

I am aware as a trainer who specializes in the communication and relationship field that much of this material now comes as second nature to me. I do believe that all trainers should practise what they preach. I will give you more examples as we proceed. Communication can be a major problem for trainers whose specialist subject is in another, usually unrelated area. This is particularly noticeable in technical trainers. Let me show you what I mean.

To communicate effectively is to connect entirely

I firmly believe that regardless of their subject discipline all trainers should be trained in the key communication skills of rapport-building. This is why it is covered in some depth on the Train-the-Trainer Master Class workshop.

Effective communication skills on all levels are a crucial requirement for anyone contemplating a career in training or teaching. When you look at the psychology profile of a genuine trainer you will discover huge similarities with that of a person in sales. When you think about it, that's what training really is, selling. You have information, skills, techniques, strategies, ideas, theories, concepts, models and tools to sell to your audience. Sometimes your audience is a willing audience (easy to sell to) and sometimes they are very unwilling (almost impossible to sell to).

The sales person has a number of products, services, add-ons, benefits and features to sell. And willing buyers are much more appreciated than the reluctant window shopper, who is determined not to part with any money.

To prove just how close these two professions are, let me ask you a question. What must sales people always sell first in order to be successful? The answer of course is themselves. This is also the answer to the same question posed to all trainers. It's a human psychology thing. People will always prefer to buy from people who either remind them of themselves or who they can relate to in some way. That, after all, is what rapport is. We hear people saying such things as, 'We're on the same wavelength' or, 'We can read each other like a book'. Unfortunately, so many trainers, those who operate in the middle ground of TRADITIONAL training, either leave out the crucial first hour of building rapport and credibility, skimp on it or get it wrong.

I remember an incident many years ago now, with a personnel officer who wanted me to develop and run a Team Leader programme. I submitted my course outline and programme notes and awaited her feedback. Her only criticism was that the introduction session was completely unnecessary, as all of the delegates knew each other. Cutting it out, she said, would save time to be used for other inputs. I diplomatically pointed out that although the delegates would know each other, I wouldn't and they wouldn't know me either.

Apart from anything else it is unfair to throw people into a learning event totally cold. In many cases the delegates need to recognize why they are there, as their managers wouldn't have briefed them sufficiently, and to get them to think about what they want to get out of the day. You also need to alleviate their fears.

Fear within the delegate is the trainer's number one enemy

One of the questions I always include in my workshop introduction sessions is the one that asks the delegates how they feel right now. Delegates are paired up and have to interview their partner ready for introduction to the whole group. I have found that it is easier for people who aren't used to attending courses to introduce someone else – it takes away the element of self-consciousness that causes people discomfort.

The response to that 'feeling' question ranges from 'worried', 'apprehensive' and 'nervous' to 'relaxed' or 'happy'. However, if the TRADITIONAL trainer is not allowing enough time for introductions or asking the right questions during the introduction then a great opportunity to build rapport and trainer credibility is being missed. People learn far more if they are free of any internal fears about an unknown event such as your training course. They also respond far more positively if they believe in the trainer.

I once co-ran a Presentation Skills course, many years ago now, when I worked as a training officer for an organization. My co-trainer was my new boss. I think it was about her allowing me to see how she trained as much as it was the other way round.

She opened the course and within five minutes went straight into the course objectives before any introductions.[3] The introductions, when they came, were not focused enough and she made the poor delegates stand at the front of the room to introduce themselves in the form of a mini-presentation.

The course then proceeded in a very business-like fashion. All of the good quality information that was delivered lacked punch and sparkle. When giving the delegates feedback, the parts of their performances that needed further work were given very formally and without sensitivity, with no encouragement and praise for any improvements made.

During one of the afternoon sessions she came over and spoke to me while the delegates were working on an activity and said, 'They don't seem to be gelling very well, I wonder what's up with them.' She surveyed the groups who were working with a growing sense of loathing and then added, 'I mean, look, no enthusiasm, I don't know.'

Sadly that was so true – she just didn't know. She didn't know why her audience were behaving the way they were. A typical TRADITIONAL trainer trait.

THEY WANT TO WOW BUT DON'T KNOW HOW

In many cases people who operate in TRADITIONAL trainer mode stick to the middle-of-the-road style of delivery because they are unsure of how to do it any differently. This comes about for a number of reasons, such as:

- They haven't observed other trainers in action.
- They have observed some other trainers but have failed to use it as a learning opportunity.
- They are more trainer focused than delegate focused.
- They take everything far too seriously.
- They lack confidence and belief in their own abilities.
- They are too self-conscious.
- They fail to practice what they preach.
- They fail to continuously develop themselves in the art of training others.
- A TRADITIONAL trainer trained them.

It is very difficult to deliver your training sessions with panache when you are feeling self-conscious and inhibited by a low sense of self-belief, or have an incorrect attitude to training and/or the delegates attending your courses. However, it is possible to deliver your hard work in a more memorable and enjoyable way. And by enjoyable I mean enjoyable for you the trainer too. Delivering with style can be learnt.

From the observations of both NIGHTMARE and TRADITIONAL trainers you can identify any traits and styles of delivery that are likely to hamper your real task. Ultimately you are there to transfer knowledge, techniques and encouragement for your delegates to go back to the workplace and implement the changes you have spent a day or two teaching. If our delegates return to work and carry on as before then we have failed in our mission. No matter what the subject matter, trainers must touch the everyday lives of their audiences.

Failing to sell the sizzle!

The main problem with TRADITIONAL trainers is that they fail to get their audience excited about the prospect of being on a training course.

Let's look at this from a different perspective by asking the question, why do most people dislike being on a training course? Answer: because they have been sent, usually without any consultation, by their boss, who inevitably will take no interest as to what they got out of attending when they return to work.

Quite often the TRADITIONAL trainer, when faced with a sea of uninterested faces, will behave in an uninterested way. They will then complain about the 'hard group' they have got. Allow me to link back here to the discussion on self-delusion and self-fulfilling prophecies. We create our own outcomes by our actions or lack of them, which is driven by our attitude of the moment.

This is where TRADITIONAL trainers really differ from the SMART trainer. The TRADITIONAL trainers' programme input sessions are trainer focused while their delivery is delegate driven – in other words, when delivering the trainer reacts to the delegates' current attitude and connected behaviours.

SMART trainers, on the other hand, reverse this, with their programme input sessions being delegate focused while their delivery leads the delegates toward the appropriate atmosphere and attitude that create positive behaviours.

This is why investing in your own development, especially in the human psychology of learning, is so critical.

People will always be willing take part in your training events if they believe that there will be a tangible benefit that will improve their lives. They want to be better, to be able to work smarter instead of just harder, they want success, they want more job satisfaction, they want enjoyment. Let's look again at the similarities with the sales person.

Today's sales person knows that customer wants are far more powerful than customer needs. Remember the two key emotions of motivation: pain and pleasure, shown here in Figure 6.1. An away motivator (a personal pain issue) becomes a catalyst for change and necessary action to ensure that change when the pain outweighs any pleasures.

Figure 6.1 *Away from pain towards pleasure*

Managers who have confrontational employees they don't know how to handle (and what manager hasn't got their share of these people?) have a pain in their working life. While this pain continues their key motivators of job satisfaction, success, etc, are under threat or non-existent. The idea here, which unfortunately is missed by TRADITIONAL and NIGHTMARE trainers alike, is to home in on this and to first emphasize the pain and then lead them toward the achievable pleasure.

With the trainer guiding delegates who are in this situation through all the rewards awaiting them when they are able to deal successfully with the confrontational and difficult employee, they are made aware of the major benefits to them personally of being on the course. Their whole attitude visibly changes. People really do love being taught how to do something better if they can see and feel the benefits of doing so.[4]

TRADITIONAL trainers mistakenly believe that they have very little or no control over the way their delegate audiences behave towards the training. By holding this belief they unwittingly create the very condition that they dread: an unresponsive audience.

I can tell you what you now already know: that you are well on your way to throwing off any lingering TRADITIONAL trainer traits and now stand poised to get practising the key SMART trainer methods. Patience is a SMART trainer virtue that is highly valuable to personal progress.

You are almost ready for Part Three, but first let's have a quick look at the SMART trainer, in Chapter 7.

The SMART trainer's summary of Chapter 6

In summary, you covered, learnt and worked on the following key factors that will help you achieve Beyond Traditional Training status by investing in your own development and becoming a SMART trainer:

- what we mean by 'TRADITIONAL trainer';
- the focus of the TRADITIONAL trainer;
- key behaviour traits of the TRADITIONAL trainer;
- the dangers of becoming safe and comfortable;
- theory is the mental bindweed that chokes TRADITIONAL trainers' courses;
- the 'talk and chalk' syndrome;
- lack of confidence through lack of control;
- time – the trainers' friend or enemy;
- communicating to connect;
- delegates' fears – the trainer's number one enemy;
- failing to sell the sizzle;
- pain and pleasure explored.

Notes

1. Manipulation in this context is positive as it builds on the chemistry that already exists within the audience group.
2. Watch out for hotels that give you break-out rooms three floors apart. This should always be deemed totally unacceptable.
3. You will learn the SMART trainer way of opening a course successfully in Chapter 7.
4. This is why the best selling books are 'How To' publications.

7

THE SMART TRAINER OBSERVED

'Fascination is one step beyond interest. Interested people want to know if it works. Fascinated people want to learn how it works.'

(Jim Rohn)

Your learning objectives in this chapter

By studying the examples, experiences and real-life case studies in this chapter you will be able to:

- recognize the critical behaviours and attitudes that the delegates of SMART trainers enjoy and benefit from;
- evaluate your own current training impact on your delegates by assessing your training style and skills against those of the SMART trainer;
- develop the next steps for a clear strategy to develop SMART trainer skills and style.

A TOUR AROUND A SMART TRAINER

So, what do SMART trainers look like? What do they sound like? What is it about them that sets them apart from the rest? Well, you're about to find out. Through this chapter/session you will have the information you need that will allow you to complete the second draft of your Action Plan.

Here are the most frequently asked questions posed on our Train-the-Trainer Master Class workshops:

- What are the critical differences that separate a SMART trainer from a TRADITIONAL one?
- How do SMART trainers design courses?
- How differently does a SMART trainer prepare for courses?
- How do SMART trainers open their training courses?
- In what way do they deliver their training sessions that makes them more effective than TRADITIONAL trainers?
- What is the SMART trainer's philosophy? (See Chapter 10)
- What are their attitudes and behaviours? (See Chapter 10)
- What keeps them so motivated?
- How do they develop their skills and strategies? (See Chapter 12)

The first five questions will be answered in this chapter and the information you gather can be used for your own development and personal improvement. I encourage you to take notes in the boxes provided so that you can refer back when you work through Chapter 8, your second Action Plan draft. So, let the session begin.

WHAT SEPARATES A SMART TRAINER FROM A TRADITIONAL ONE?

There are many differences between these two trainers. We won't compare them with NIGHTMARE trainers for, as you will have gathered when you went through that session, they really are in a league of their own. The journey from NIGHTMARE trainer to SMART trainer, while possible, can be a long and arduous one, whereas from TRADITIONAL to SMART is a manageable process over a relatively short period. I don't mean it will be an overnight transition – habits, both physical and mental, take a little longer than that to change. If certain 'holding back' traits are recognized and acknowledged, then with a little planning and practice, something all SMART trainers undertake, a transition from one side of the line to the other isn't far away.

As I mentioned earlier, there can be many differences that separate the TRADITIONAL trainer and SMART trainer, but sometimes the differences are quite small. Sometimes a person can be a borderline

SMART trainer and maybe one or two behaviours or beliefs let him or her down. You will now see a number of key comparisons with what SMART trainers do that gives them that status, and experience the actions of trainers that have let themselves and their delegates or clients down. As you will see, all of the errors can be easily removed from the way we normally train. One of the critical differences between the two trainers is that of focus. So let's explore that for a moment.

The vast majority of people are locked into the habit of inward focus. Inward focus is OK for certain self-development tasks as these are done over relatively short periods of time, but the real problem lies in the fact that most people work and live in a virtually permanent state of inward focus. Hang on a minute, I hear you saying, just what exactly is inward focus? Surely focus is focus, isn't it? Well, no it isn't. Allow me to explain.

Inward focus is just what it says. You are focused on your feelings, your situation, your outcomes, your pain, your pleasure, your gain, your loss and anything else that has either a direct or indirect impact on you and your life. As I've mentioned, some inward focus is essential for personal progress and growth, but any more inward focus than is required for this is really pure indulgence.

Inward focus is the cause of most of our worries, fears and failures. When I run my Powerful Presentations Master Class, I train the delegates to divert their focus away from themselves and their particular situation and personal feelings of the moment, when they are going to deliver a presentation.

What happens to a problem that you are experiencing, when you dwell on it for any length of time? It grows, usually out of all proportion to the reality of the situation you face. It is where the saying, 'Making a mountain out of a molehill' came from. And why is it that when we talk to someone we can trust about our awful problem, we begin to see it for what it really is, this little insignificant molehill of an issue and not the mountain of doom and gloom we set ourselves up for? The person we are talking to, sometimes wittingly, most times purely by chance, gets us to change our perspective. We begin to move away from being inward focused, to becoming outward focused and looking at the bigger picture and its implications and possibilities.

To become outward focused there is an important technique to learn. The good news is it is easy to learn, even easier to practise, can be practised anywhere at anytime and is instantly effective. Here are some examples of how it can work for you. I encourage you to try it when preparing for your next training course.

The outward focus technique

When preparing a training course, workshop, seminar or presentation, draw up a list of all the benefits that your audience will gain through the experience. Write down as many as you can think of, no matter how small or trivial they may appear to you. Remember, SMART trainers don't make assumptions about their audiences – what appears trivial to you could well be a critical factor in someone else's life, so give it the respect it deserves.

If you're having trouble putting together a decent sized list then survey a few people and get some different perspectives and ideas to add to your own. Quite often a fresh approach from someone else can be quite enlightening. Once you have got your list spend a few moments really familiarizing yourself with it and then think of why each individual in your audience deserves to receive these benefits.

Then think about the success they will enjoy if the skills and techniques you are imparting are acted upon. The benefits the content of your workshop or seminar will bring to every participant who will attend. The inspiration your energetic and charismatic delivery will generate within each one of your course delegates. Work at creating within yourself a strong desire to make every single member of your audience successful. Visualize and experience all of these things.

Now, this is where the power of this technique really lies. The reason it works and is so powerful is because it is part of the 'universal law' of sowing and reaping. In Chapter 8 I will take you through all of the most critical universal laws and then teach you how best to use them. In the meantime, let's continue.

Sowing and reaping, also known as 'what goes around comes around', is something we experience all of the time, whether we are aware of it or not, and most people remain ignorant of this. For years now I have lived and worked to the philosophy of 'your success is my success'. You see, the more people I can help become successful and the more successful I can help them become, the more success I receive.

The power of sharing

Another fundamental difference between TRADITIONAL and SMART trainers is that one teaches while the other shares. SMART trainers have learnt that if they share a new skill or piece of knowledge the recipient will still learn from the initial sharing but will have their interest raised and will want to learn even more. The key difference here is that SMART trainers are constantly working on their own development and this is where sharing becomes really powerful. The best explanation I ever heard of this was from one of the self-development masters I have mentioned before, the great Jim Rohn. He says that sharing is the best action you can do for your own self-improvement. He explains it this way.

When you have learnt something new, like a skill, technique or strategy, then create an urge in yourself that compels you to share it with as many people as you can, so that they may benefit from it too. Imagine if you were to share your discovery with 10 people. Each one of those 10 will hear it once, whereas you have now heard it another 10 times. The people you have shared your discovery with have gained, but you have gained 10-fold. You give to others and you receive benefits back. Everybody wins.

SMART trainers work to this strategy all of the time. It is a fundamental part of their 'your success is my success' philosophy. It's enjoyable to do and it works. It is all part of the outward focus. It also has a powerful calming effect for people new to presenting. In the presentation skills preparation sessions during our workshops we teach delegates to use the outward focus method to gain control of their nerves and anxiety.

Public speaking nerves are entirely due to a high concentration of inward focus. If we are not careful we not only feel those butterflies flying crazily in our stomachs, we swear we can see, hear and smell them too. This is not good for our composure and for keeping a clear head. We want so badly to soar to the heights of success, yet we only seem able to picture crashing and burning in front of a stunned audience. Oh, the punishment we heap onto ourselves. What are we to do? Well, do what the SMART trainer does – change your focus. Don't think about poor me, think about lucky them. While preparing the presentation your thoughts should be on the benefits each member of the audience will receive, how much useful information they will receive. Your audience is so lucky that they are to be addressed by someone who genuinely cares for their wellbeing and future success.

We tell our delegates to keep the focus on the audience at every stage of the preparation. And when they are standing there, composing themselves ready for the start of their talk, they need to be saying in the privacy of their minds just how much they really want every member of their audience to succeed and benefit. This mental talk needs to be totally sincere and genuine. When they have done this, delegates have reported during the feedback sessions that they felt that the audience was with them all the way. That the audience came across as warm and encouraging and consequently they then relaxed even more and gained confidence, which enhanced their performance even further.

This was because of another universal law: the law of like attracting like. Think of a time when you were a member of an audience. If the speaker came across as genuine and sincere, didn't you automatically warm to them, to begin to like them? You see, powerful stuff doesn't have to be difficult to use.

HOW DO SMART TRAINERS DESIGN COURSES?

In addition to adopting the 'outward focus' approach, SMART trainers are also highly organized and methodical in their approach to design and planning. They leave nothing to chance and use the skill of anticipation, amongst others. They also use copious amounts of tried and tested methods that people can actually try out for themselves, delivered in digestible chunks in a logical way. Sounds easy – well it is, as you will now discover.

SMART trainers always begin with the end in mind. Exactly what is it that this course, workshop or presentation wants to achieve? They create a written goal that is as specific as possible. This enables them to really picture, hear and feel what the end result will look and sound like. You can begin your preparation without this but you won't get very far before you hit difficulties. I mean, how can you successfully plan a route if you are unsure of your destination?

The big four questions

In order to get into the position of creating a specific overall objective for your training event, you need to ask yourself and work your way through the four key questions, often referred to as 'the big four questions'. They are:

1. What do I want my delegates to know, or do, as a result of the training?
2. What is the best way to impart this training?

3. Who is the best person to carry out this training, if not me?
4. How can I reinforce this training?

By answering question one in as much detail as possible you will be in a position to draft a clearly defined objective for your training. As you work through the rest of the design you will then go to the next questions in turn. You will experience this as you work through this chapter and Part Three of your programme.

Course design in action

When I'm designing an event, whether a one-day workshop or a 12-month development programme, I write the final draft of the overall objective on an index card and keep it in view the whole time. This makes it easy for me to check the materials I have selected for the workshop against it in order to put the material into one of three categories:

1. definite insertion;
2. possible insertion;
3. throw it out.

I have to say, from personal experience, it can be quite hard leaving something out if it is one of your favourite activities, simulations or exercises. You have to be disciplined, but at the end of the day if it doesn't move the delegates towards that desired outcome then it deserves no place in your programme, no matter how brilliant or zappy the piece may be.

So, with the end result written at least in draft form (remember, nothing is cast in stone – it is quite OK to fine-tune your overall course objective as your design progresses) then begin to gather all of the available pieces of information, theories, concepts and models together that relate to that subject, and those that interlink and overlap. Then look for the activities that are available that will enable you to put as much activity into the course as possible.[1] This, the SMART trainer knows, will help the delegates to make sense of the theories and concepts and to remember them longer.

Once you have gathered all of your potential material, and of course there will be far more than you could ever fit into the time frame of the course, you can then move onto the material selection process.

If you are satisfied with the desired outcome of the training event you can then use that as a template against which to check training inputs. For instance, will this activity move my delegates towards this outcome, will this input session give them the necessary information they need to practise the actual 'how tos' of putting the new skill or technique into action back at the workplace?

Then you write up the heading and key details of each session you are proposing to run, either on index cards, Post-it Notes (easier than index cards) or using a computer software program (easiest of all). With this done you can then manipulate the sessions to find the best logical order, as it would come across to your target audience (outward focus).

The anticipation that you exercise is again connected to the outward focus process, this time through the communication skill of empathy. SMART trainers will continually be putting themselves into the 'shoes' of their target audience as they work on their design, having gathered as much information as possible through previous meetings or telephone calls with the appropriate people. As they design their programme they ask questions as if they were one of the potential delegates. Examples of such questions would be:

- Is this particular input session pitched at the right level for this type of audience?
- Does it explain the process in the right language for this audience?
- Does it explain the process in enough detail, or too much detail?
- Does it insult their intelligence?
- If I were experiencing this activity for the first time would it strike me as degrading, frivolous, nonsense, or fun and informative?
- Would this input session raise more questions than it answers?
- What type of questions would this input session produce from this audience?
- What are the likely questions I would ask if faced with this information for the first time? (Write each one of them down for future preparation.)

The whole exercise is designed to maximize the SMART trainers' readiness so that they minimize the chances of being wrong-footed. If as many 'anticipated' questions and queries can be designed into the programme as possible then it enhances the whole experience for both the delegate and the trainer. And when something is thrown at the

SMART trainers that they failed to anticipate,[2] guess what? That's right, they have a strategy for dealing with that too.

HOW DO SMART TRAINERS PREPARE FOR COURSES?

They prepare by leaving absolutely nothing to chance and trusting no one. They work to a checklist that will contain all of the items that they will need to run a successful workshop. Their checklist is a tangible object that they physically use each time. The consequences of failing to do this can be quite painful and costly.

A TRADITIONAL trainer (who was borderline SMART) let himself and others down when he failed the checklist test and suffered both physically and financially; most probably his reputation took a bit of a knock too. This trainer was running a series of workshops for a large client that took him all around Britain. The workshops were quite innovative and consisted of delegates checking their learning and understanding through a series of quizzes played on a giant board game that measured about 4 foot by 3 foot. The board came as a kit of four large quadrants that slotted together and as you can imagine took up quite a bit of room in his car.

The courses were running back to back on many occasions, which kept him away from home for days at a time. He also ran a different workshop for this company and they wanted him to run it in North Wales and then the workshop with the giant board game up in Glasgow. He got himself prepared for four days away from home and two workshops running back to back.

He had a successful two days in North Wales and then travelled up to Scotland, arriving at the hotel at 9 o'clock in the evening. He met up with the owner of the training company with whom he was going to co-run the workshop. They decided it would be best to set up everything that night and then relax over a nightcap and discuss the next day's programme. It was just as well that they did.

To his horror he discovered that he had failed to load the giant board pieces into his car. He had left them leaning up against the wall in his office in Derby. Of course the owner of the training company, while not exactly impressed, could sympathize but insisted that they needed the boards to run the workshop, as this was the pivotal activity. He had no choice but to drive through the night back down to Derby, collect the forgotten boards and drive back up in time for the start of the workshop at 9 am the next morning.

If anything could emphasize just how critical working to a checklist is then it is the sorry tale of this trainer. It was definitely a problem that was preventable. And this is why SMART trainers use checklists.

Prepare a checklist for every course you run and have it laminated and placed with the course materials however you may store them. It's professional, it's easy and it saves time, money and grey hairs.

I mentioned trusting no one, and this next case study explains my point. It concerns an individual who displayed alarming TRADITIONAL trainer tendencies that could have indicated that he was a borderline NIGHTMARE trainer. When setting up your training room do not, and I repeat this without apology, *do not* allow other people to set up the equipment, at least not without making sure that you check it over before the session begins. This TRADITIONAL trainer incident concerns an extremely experienced training manager and chair of the school governors where these two days were being held. Here's what happened, some years ago, to this hapless chap, much to his total embarrassment and his audience's total delight.

It was the opening of a two-day workshop for sixth-formers designed as an introduction to the world of work. I was there as a facilitator representing the company I then worked for, as we had an active Industry/Education Links programme. These were normally quite boisterous events due to the audience but were great fun for both the students and facilitators alike. Everybody involved benefited from the programme.

The opening session was to set the scene and explain the key elements of the next two days. The trainer had prepared, back at his company office on the latest equipment, a set of the flashiest overhead slides (laptop-based slide shows were still prohibitively expensive and anyway this guy was a TRADITIONAL trainer so he wouldn't have been interested in such modern technology). Everything was set up and ready to roll. One hundred and fifty 16- to 18-year-olds were crammed into the school hall. The sound of talking, shouting, giggling and tomfoolery filled the large room. The overhead projector was in place and our trainer was stood next to it surveying his audience.

He called for silence and after a few minutes achieved this, and began his introduction to the workshop. After he had been talking for about five minutes, having built up a great expectation to the slide show that was to follow, he carefully placed the first full-colour slide on to the projector. He talked some more, preparing his audience for what this slide would be showing. His hand was hovering over the on switch; 300 eyes were fixed on the large white screen waiting for the burst of light along with the annoying rattle of the projector fan. He turned his head towards the screen and threw the switch. Nothing happened. He flicked it on and off repeatedly, but to no avail. He continued staring at the screen for a while as if in total shock or performing some form of psychic technique that would produce the light as if by magic. However, it turned out to be shock followed by disbelief.

I quickly looked at the OHP to see if I could establish the problem. And I had no problem in spotting it, for not only was the projector not plugged in, the lead was still wound tight around the storage lugs. I knew immediately that he had assumed that whoever had promised to set up the hall for his presentation had got everything working. Oh! How naïve. How foolish. How TRADITIONAL trainer.

Oops! Sorry, I forgot to prepare myself, but it's only you

This incident, which I have used many times as a prime example on my Train-the-Trainer Master Class workshops, is a wonderful example of how the key behaviours and attitudes that the SMART trainer always works to can ensure you always have a professional approach.

Our TRADITIONAL trainer's faux pas tells us many things about him. They reveal the darker side of the training profession, which is why I want to eradicate it so badly. This type of behaviour gives all trainers a bad name. Let's, briefly, break down this trainer's misdemeanour and learn from it.

He allowed someone else to set up the equipment. Although this is no great sin in itself – after all, many of us are very busy and welcome assistance in this area – it was his lack of professionalism that let him down. The error was in the lack of care over whether the equipment was set up correctly. Equipment can be set up by someone else who knows a great deal less about it than the trainer. They may not even check that it works and not care too much whether it does work or not. Remember that they most probably will be nowhere near your training event when the awful discovery is made. In a nutshell, it ain't them stood up in front of the audience. This is why this strategy is never a sound one to use.

He didn't check anything at all. The fact that he only discovered that the projector was not working when he went to show the first slide tells us that he hadn't even thought it important enough to ensure it would be in focus when it plastered the slides contents on to the screen. Which also tells us that he hadn't checked that the screen was in the correct position, or that it could be seen by all the students sat around the hall.

This whole episode came about because he didn't care enough about his audience, which in turn tells us he was totally inward focused. And that much inward focus is considered an overdose by SMART trainers. It causes the illness known as 'arrogant ineptitude'. So remember: check everything and trust no one.

HOW DO SMART TRAINERS OPEN THEIR TRAINING COURSES?

With a bang! And not just a blank screen. Starting your training events with a bang is essential because all audiences need to have their interest hooked as quickly as possible. You can do this without the aid of pyrotechnics or any other special effects.

It links up with sharing. SMART trainers want to share all of the great techniques and strategies that they know work, but because most people come into the training room as passive attendees they will need working on and warming up before any learning can take place.

SMART trainers have an acute understanding of the human motivation process. They know that you cannot force people to want to learn. They also know that just as people hate being sold to, they hate being talked at and taught at. SMART trainers will be aware that people attending their courses will bring with them a mixture of attitudes and beliefs and each delegate will fall into one of the following attitude/belief groups:

- sent by their manager but haven't got a clue why;
- believe they know everything there is to know already;
- know why they've been sent but can't see the connection with their job;
- believe they're too old to learn anything new;
- know why they've been sent but believe they are already competent;

- believe training is something that happens to other people;
- believe that admitting to needing training is tantamount to failure;
- realize that self-development is a continuous process.

Your audience will be a mixture of these and possibly more, so complex is the human psyche, but SMART trainers do need to understand and appreciate the power of people's beliefs as it is these beliefs that drive their behaviours.

With those beliefs rolling around in the minds of their audience, SMART trainers know that they have to persuade their audience to want to listen, join in and learn for themselves. So what is the trigger that creates this attitude and subsequent behaviour? In a word, 'benefits'. Everybody buys benefits and will often pay handsomely for the ones that they believe they really must have. SMART trainers do what all successful sales people do: they sell the benefits of being there, asking questions, joining in with the examples and learning so that what has been learnt can be used back at the workplace.

Once people can see what's in it for them and that you genuinely want to help them achieve that benefit as quickly as possible, then they become active learners and not passive attendees. This is why SMART trainers do not skimp over the introduction and scene-building sessions. In showbusiness this is known as the 'warm-up session'. If you've ever been a member of a TV studio audience for a comedy show you will know that a warm-up person gets the audience ready to receive the main show. Your training course is the same. You want your delegates primed ready for the lessons that will teach them the new skills they are there to learn. SMART trainers know that relaxed and happy people are far more receptive to new ideas, learn faster and remember information longer.

SMART trainers also believe that the two 'Ls' go together: learning and laughter. Learning should be fun and free of pain. Your outward focus is also on the delegates' enjoyment of the whole learning experience. When people are involved in the learning experience and enjoying it then two things happen. Time seems to pass more quickly and they retain more new information.

While I encourage you to adopt your own style of opening, there will be a few examples of openings and the techniques used in Part Three of your Master Class programme for you to study and adapt for yourself.

HOW DO SMART TRAINERS DELIVER THEIR TRAINING SESSIONS?

How many ways are there? If you don't know the answer to that question then you haven't explored the possibilities enough. The main guideline for SMART trainer delivery is through minimum trainer inputs and maximum 'hands-on' activities, whatever form these may take. These different methods allow the delegates to experience the ideas, methods, skills or strategies for themselves.

There is an ancient saying that goes:

I hear and I forget.
I see and I remember.
I do and I understand.

SMART trainers work to this at all times and design their programme to deliver this as much as is possible. People crave involvement; they want to be part of the action even when they're telling you that they will never take part in a role-play.

Delegates are unaware of their love for role-plays

Remember the four stages of learning? Well, our delegates are very much in that first stage when they attend your training course – unconscious incompetence. They don't know that they don't know what role-play really is or whether or not they will actually enjoy it.

Now, TRADITIONAL and NIGHTMARE trainers can cause damage here if these activities and their delegates' fears of them are not handled correctly. The key is to sell the idea of the activity well in advance of it happening, emphasizing the benefits and the fun in doing it. Forcing someone to do something on a training course is always forbidden in the rules of SMART training.

To demonstrate that delegate unawareness exists I will share with you an experience I had quite recently. I carried out a number of communication skills workshops for a large company in Scotland. All delegates were engineers and very pragmatic and down to earth. They made it quite clear to me during the needs analysis interviews I carried out that they did not want role-plays. They said they were unrealistic, embarrassing and bore no relation to their day-to-day work.

I was running four one-day workshops with 12 managers on each. The first two workshops were run in a well-equipped training room with a break-out room. I put them through the simulations, which are a variation on the role-play method. The evaluation sheets of a few of the delegates indicated that they found the role-plays the least effective.

On the third day I was moved due to some internal event and got a room that was much smaller and not so well equipped, and had no break-out room. With 12 delegates this made role-plays virtually impossible, so I went to my contingency plan for such times and used a different activity and showed a corresponding video instead. The evaluation forms from this workshop revealed in the box, 'What areas of the workshop could have been increased?' that a number of delegates would like to have had role-plays. Damned if you do, damned if you don't.

How to get delegates to take part in role-plays will be explored in detail in Part Three. You will also learn, through some classic real-life examples, how NIGHTMARE and TRADITIONAL trainers compound the problems through their insensitivity and ignorance of delegate motivators.

There are a variety of ways to approach the core activities of training events. You will learn more about these and how to actually use them in Part Three of this book. After the summary of this lesson we'll be ready to tackle the next crucial stage of becoming a SMART trainer.

The SMART trainer's summary of Chapter 7

In summary, you covered, learnt and worked on the following key factors that will help you achieve Beyond Traditional Training status by investing in your own development and becoming a SMART trainer:

- a tour around a SMART trainer;
- discovered the most commonly asked questions;
- learnt what separates a SMART trainer from a TRADITIONAL one;
- introduced to the outward focus technique;
- discovered the power of sharing;
- learnt how SMART trainers design programmes;
- learnt how SMART trainers prepare for their training events;
- learnt how SMART trainers open their training events;
- learnt how SMART trainers deliver some key elements of their training;
- discovered through real-life examples a number of ways not to train.

Notes

1. Nothing is new in training; only the angle it is approached from can be altered. You will discover how to avoid reinventing the wheel and saving yourself up to 80 per cent on preparation time in Chapter 12.
2. SMART trainers, while being the epitome of professionalism, are human too.

8

BUILDING ON THE FOUNDATIONS OF YOUR ACTION PLAN – ACTION PLAN PART II

'Don't let learning from your own experiences take too long. If you have been doing wrong for the last 10 years, I would suggest that's long enough.'

(Jim Rohn)

Your learning objectives in this chapter

By following the directions, ideas and suggestions in this chapter, you will have learnt how to:

- consolidate the key learning points achieved so far;
- recognize and be able to use the universal laws that govern your personal development and training success;
- develop further your step-by-step Action Plan for SMART trainer status;
- produce a list of key actions to follow for achieving peak performance in training preparation and delivery.

In order to successfully complete the above objectives, work your way through this chapter, noting down where indicated all relevant information. You will be referring back to this collection of information during your final Action Plan preparation. You will also find it useful in the future when using this programme to assess how you are progressing. Remember, if you need any clarification or have any questions that you feel you need answered then please do not hesitate to contact me for guidance.

Let's now work on through this brief session in readiness for the final part of your journey to SMART trainer status and true training professionalism.

THE 10 KEY SMART TRAINER SKILLS

As a reminder, here is the list of key SMART trainer skills that you worked with in Part One:

1. active listening;
2. questioning techniques;
3. handling conflict and confrontation;
4. building rapport (NLP, body language, communication);
5. self-organization/self-management;
6. negotiation techniques;
7. influencing and persuasion skills;
8. motivational techniques;
9. facilitation skills;
10. observation skills.

You will be looking at these skills in more detail during Part Three of your programme. It will be at this point that you will be taken through the key elements of each one. When you do this you will then be able to determine how you can further build on your strengths and eliminate any weaknesses. From this you will have a very clear set of actions to follow on your Action Plan.

THE CONSOLIDATION PROCESS

As in all learning, before you can move on to the next chunk of new material you must ensure that you have fully grasped and can relate to the information you have gathered so far. The best way of doing this is to spend a little time making some key notes of the learning you have just been through.

To assist you in this it is best to go through the simple structure below. This guides you through a small series of key questions that will enable you to pull everything together so that it all makes real sense. It will also enhance your understanding of how best to go about changing what you have discovered you need to change. Let's have a look at these questions and gather the information that we can call on as we progress through the last section of your PDP.

THE CONSOLIDATION QUESTIONS

Please answer the following questions briefly in the boxes provided.

What have you discovered about asking questions of yourself in line with designing your training courses?

What did you find most useful about the 'outward focus' technique?

What separates the SMART trainer from the TRADITIONAL trainer?

What are your current views on the power of sharing?

List at least two actions that you propose to do differently with regard to designing your training programmes.

List at least two actions that you propose to do differently with regard to preparing your training programmes.

List at least two actions that you propose to do differently with regard to opening your training programmes.

What do you propose to change first with regard to how you currently operate as a training professional?

YOUR PERSONAL ROUTE TO SMART TRAINER STATUS – SECOND DRAFT

You are now ready to move on to the second part of your PDP. This framework allows you to pull together all of the key pieces of information about your current training abilities and what you want to achieve in the coming months and years.

This time you can use the information you have gained from the three earlier chapters in this part of the book. Again, I must emphasize the importance of making an honest assessment of your current training style and performance levels. Have you always had the best possible attitude towards your delegates, your client's needs, the impact you have on others? Have your training behaviours been consistent with SMART trainer behaviours?

In the tables below re-write or fine-tune your self-appraisal list, adding comments and suggestions as you go. Remember it is your own personal and private plan; no one else will see this unless you choose to show them.

All of the following frameworks and structures will be referred back to as you progress on to the successful conclusion of this Master Class workshop in a book. In Part Three, you will complete your third and final draft of your Action Plan for becoming a SMART trainer. So, get out your pen or pencil again and complete the following sections as specifically as you can.

Re-visiting the three frameworks for achieving SMART trainer status

The three frameworks will enable you to focus all your energies in the right direction and on the critical elements. With the help of the previous three chapters and what you have completed in this chapter so far, you can map out your route accurately. Once you have completed Table 8.1 as far as you can, move on to the second framework.

Time to revisit your findings for your PDP

You can now update the information in each of the areas within this framework. List again, in Table 8.2, all the appropriate information that you have collected through the previous input session in this section.

Table 8.1 *Framework 1*

Skill levels, attitudes and behaviours I have identified as being an obstacle to achieving my goal of SMART trainer	*Key recommendations required to initiate improvement in my performance and effectiveness as a trainer*

The information you store here will be useful reference material as you complete the blueprint of your PDP. Table 8.3 is the document of key activities that you will put into action to guarantee your SMART trainer status as quickly as possible.

THE UNIVERSAL LAWS EXPLORED BRIEFLY

Universal laws exist. We can see evidence of this as we go about our day-to-day tasks. We experience good things and bad things. We have

Table 8.2 *Framework 2*

Current Assets

Strengths	*Key skills used*

Identified Potential

Hidden strengths to develop	*New skills/knowledge required*

Key Changes That Need to Occur

Attitude/behaviours displayed	*Changes recommended*

successes and we have failures. What we have to learn is that while there is such a thing as 'luck' that can intervene in our lives and change it in a massive way, most of what we experience is created by our own actions or inactions. The universal laws will always be. And even if you stubbornly refuse to believe in any of it, that won't matter one jot. This is because believing in the universal laws is not a prerequisite for them to work and affect your life.

Table 8.3 *Framework 3*

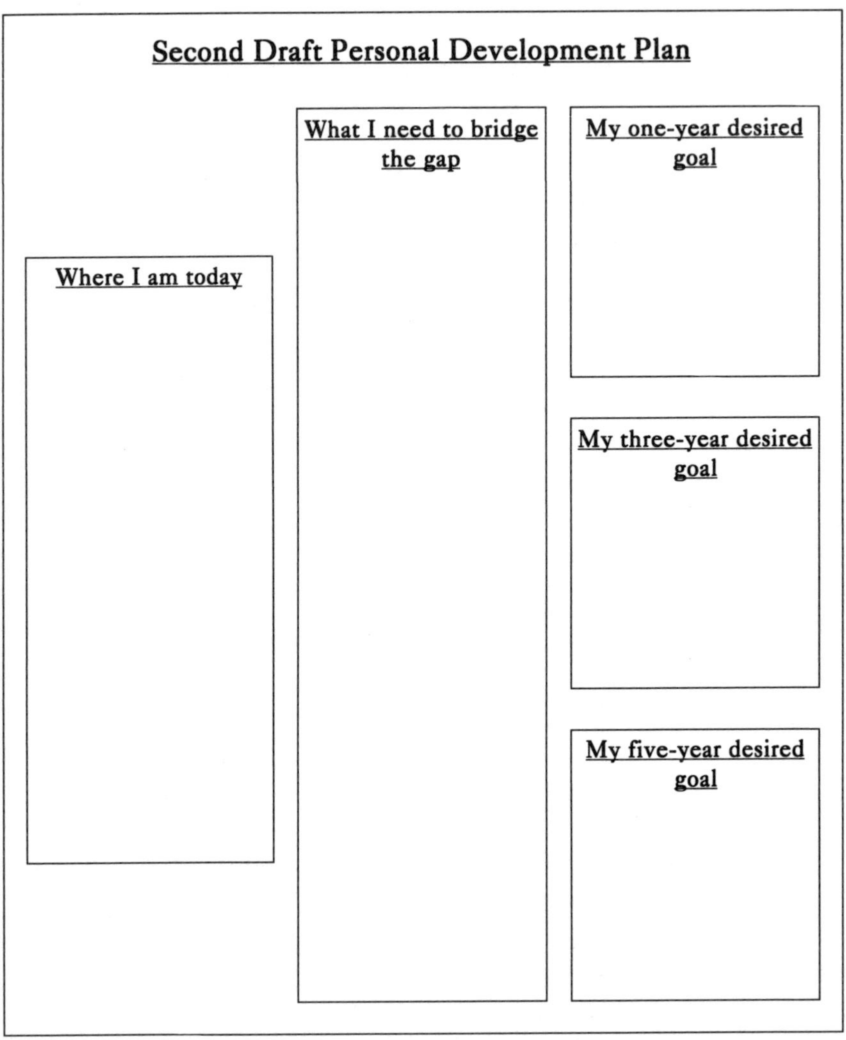

The key to working with the universal laws is awareness – of what they are and what they affect. Some you will be familiar with, and even if you think it is a load of old mumbo jumbo you will have experience of the outcomes of such laws that leave a dusting of doubt within your mind.

I am going to ask you, like I ask all of my delegates, to remain open minded and to suspend judgement while you are exploring these laws.

I am not asking you to buy them; as I've said, not believing in them doesn't stop them from working, just examine the evidence and decide for yourself.

This isn't the place to go into masses of detail about universal laws and there are publications where you can research this for yourself. My intention is to just let you in on some major possibilities. I discovered these laws through my own self-development and I want to share the key elements of that information with you. There are many universal laws. Here I discuss four of them and how they can be acted upon in the realm of the SMART trainer. They can be studied in more depth through Deepak Chopra's book, *The Seven Spiritual Laws of Success*, which I have drawn on for this example:

- The law of cause and effect.
- The law of giving and receiving.
- The law of least effort.
- The law of intention and desire.

I will now give you a brief overview of each of these. Work at placing these with experiences you have encountered throughout your life.

The law of cause and effect

Every action generates a force of energy that returns to us in kind; in other words what we sow is what we reap. It ties in with the process of 'behaviour breeds behaviour'. We know from experience that if someone is rude, angry and generally off with us for no apparent reason we tend to be the same towards them.

The law of giving and receiving

Life consists of flows of energy. Exchange creates its own flow of energy, as there are different aspects of the flow of energy in the universe. In order to gain more we have to give more. This ties in with our power of sharing. I give people skills, techniques and strategies in order to improve their lives; in return I gain from this experience.

I feel good about helping people and if I genuinely want them to achieve success then I will ensure that my skills and knowledge are always at a level that is relevant. In return I also receive recommendations and referrals for my work. As all of the laws interlink and entwine with one another I also enjoy the positive outcomes of the law of cause and effect – sowing and reaping.

As proof that this works, I can tell you that in the five years that I have been running my own consultancy company I have never spent a single penny on advertising. Every work project has been through word-of-mouth referral.

The law of least effort

Do less and accomplish more. There are three components to the law of least effort. The first is acceptance. This means that you make a commitment to accept people, situations and circumstances as they occur. For instance, when you feel frustrated or upset by a person or a situation, you are not reacting to the person or situation but to your feelings about the person or situation. You have a choice about how you decide to feel about it. The law of least effort says let those negative feelings go and things will move on and progress.

Accepting the more negative delegates on your courses as the truth of the situation, you remain more objective and therefore more in control and able to see other possibilities in moving them closer to the desired outcome.

The law of intention and desire

Conscious change is brought about by the two qualities inherent in consciousness: attention and intention. Attention energizes, and intention transforms. Whatever you put your attention on will grow stronger in your life. Now we know this is true of both positive and negative aspects. We have all experienced what happens when we dwell on a problem: it grows bigger and seems worse than it really is. (Remember the mountains out of molehills analogy.) Whatever you take your attention away from will wither and die – paying no attention to your children's pet goldfish for instance!

Intention, on the other hand, triggers transformation of energy and information. Intention organizes its own fulfilment. We can all relate to a time when the intention to change jobs or buy a new car became so strong that we created enough energy and gathered enough new information to make it happen.

I extend my warmest thanks and give full acknowledgement to Deepak Chopra whose work I have studied with much fascination and great success. Expanding our knowledge and awareness is essential for our continual development and progress. So please create the desire to keep on learning your craft with the intention of putting it all into practice for the good of others. You will then reap what you sow and enjoy the rewards that you deserve.

ACTION IS THE KEY

There is a 10-word saying, where each of the 10 words contains just two letters. This small sentence says it all in terms of personal achievement and success:

> If it is to be, it is up to me.

That's right – no one else will make it happen for you. If you want to improve and progress and achieve recognition within your profession as an authority on the training, development and success of others, then you hold the key.

Placing the key into the lock and turning those levers so that the door will open is the action. Do you desire to become the best trainer that you could possibly be? Pay attention to the information you require and what you need to do and then make it your intention to make it happen.

In light of what you have learnt and discovered so far, spend a few minutes to write down in Table 8.4 the actions you intend to carry out to begin your own upgraded self-development journey. Once you have completed this little exercise you will have successfully completed Part Two of this programme. Well done! Now have a break and move on to the last section where you will progress even closer to becoming a SMART trainer who operates Beyond Traditional Training with relative ease.

Table 8.4 *The key actions I intend to carry out immediately*

1.	2.
3.	4.
5.	6.
7.	8.
9.	10.
11.	12.

The SMART trainer's summary of Chapter 8

In summary, you covered, learnt and worked on the following key factors that will help you achieve Beyond Traditional Training status by investing in your own development and becoming a SMART trainer:

- the 10 key SMART trainer skills;
- the consolidation process and questions;
- second draft of your PDP;
- some universal laws.

PART THREE

PUTTING IT ALL INTO PRACTICE

'How long should I try? Until.'

(Jim Rohn)

ACTION IS THE KEY

In this section your focus will be guided towards total action. You will be introduced to a variety of training methods and tools and the philosophy that make up the SMART trainer's armoury. Through the chapters you will discover the steps you need to take to successfully complete your Personal Development Plan.

Three of the next four chapters will show you key behaviours, attitudes and actions that are displayed and demonstrated by all SMART trainers and that have an impact on the delegates in the training room and the clients' bottom line. There will obviously be minor behaviours, which you will be introduced to, but during these sessions we will concentrate on teaching you how to implement the major ones.

Success by the inch is a cinch, by the yard it's hard

SMART trainers are, amongst other things, realists. You will not achieve everything overnight. You will need to pace yourself and remain patient. The whole process does not take that long if you apply the actions you have discovered you need to take.

You will be in a position by the end of this book to put into practice many key behaviours that separate the SMART from the TRADITIONAL trainer. You will receive immediate benefits from training with these methods and working with upgraded attitudes and mental software. You deserve it and what's even more important, your delegates deserve it. The training profession needs it; in fact it demands it. There really is a desperate need for better trainers out there. You are now close to becoming one of those.

Remember: you are not alone.

All SMART trainers believe in exceeding their delegates' and clients' expectations. The Americans call it 'going the extra mile' and interestingly enough that extra mile is never crowded. You will be one of the elite few who really care enough about their profession to work and live to the principles of being 'in the service of others'.

SMART trainers are never satisfied with how they are performing. They are always hungry for improvement, for achieving that incremental advantage over the competition for the good of the profession as a whole. It's that little bit of inward focus that we are allowed. With this striving for excellence, fantastic things happen. Delegates receive a higher standard of training; their performance improves by larger steps and lasts for longer; the clients receive a great return on their investment; and the profession grows in stature through its improving levels of integrity and professionalism. That is a recap of my vision; incorporate into your own and join me in becoming the SMART trainer that I know you are capable of being.

The four chapters in this section are:

9. How to become a SMART trainer;
10. The SMART trainer's philosophy and professional attitude;
11. How SMART trainers present themselves;
12. The SMART trainer methods for you to action – Action Plan Part III.

This part of the book is equivalent to day three of the Master Class workshop. Keep your mind open and alert. If you feel the need to refer back to previous sections and draft action plans, please do. Break off and practise any key methods when you feel it would be appropriate to do so.

The third and final part of your programme will now commence. Continue to take notes and highlight key areas for quick future reference. Let's begin.

9

HOW TO BECOME A SMART TRAINER

'To attract attractive people, you must become attractive.
To attract powerful people, you must become powerful.
To attract committed people, you must be committed.
Instead of going to work on them, you go to work on yourself.
If you become, you can attract.'

(Jim Rohn)

Your learning objectives in this chapter

By studying the examples, recorded experiences and real-life case studies in this chapter you will have:

- discovered the principles and strategies of the SMART trainer through the 'code of practice';
- learnt the key behaviours, methods and techniques that produce SMART trainer performance;
- evaluated your own current training impact by comparing what you do know with how the SMART trainer operates.

This chapter will introduce you to the 'code of practice' that all SMART trainers operate to at all times. You were introduced to it briefly earlier in the programme during the introduction. It was the acronym SMART TRAINER, and you will be learning the activities and behaviours behind each of the elements.

This code, also known as the agenda, is what SMART trainers have found to be the golden rules of training when it comes to delivering training events that go beyond the TRADITIONAL methods. As you work your way through each of the elements below you will see how together they produce the overall effect of the SMART training methodology.

The SMART trainer's philosophies, attitudes and behaviours for which this is the framework will then follow. It is by working through this structured framework that you will begin to develop the positive habits of the SMART trainer and all of the rewards and success that brings.

You will see as you work your way through the remaining chapters of this part of the book that the elements of the framework build on each other, interlink with one another and develop into a major strategy of positive attitudes, thinking habits and actions.

So, as you go through each of the elements of the framework I want you to visualize yourself using the methods as you are training and preparing to train. Really picture yourself carrying out each of the methods and begin to raise your awareness of how it feels, how it would sound like with you acting on them with your delegates, and how it would look with you running your training events or conducting your business in this way. Please begin so that you can prepare yourself for the remaining chapters and your Action Plan for SMART trainer status.

REVISITING THE AGENDA

This would be a good place to revisit your agenda in becoming a SMART trainer. Let us go through your personal SMART TRAINER guide and explore a bit more of the detail of each of the segments. I'm taking you back to the introduction now and the SMART TRAINER acronym. If we explore each element and clarify the critical components and how they work, you then begin to see the picture of the puzzle emerging from all of the individual pieces.

Through this chapter and the remaining three in this part of the book you will learn exactly how to perform as a SMART trainer for most of the time. Remember peak performance is your personal best consistently delivered. This means of course that over time you learn new techniques and skills and practise them until competent. You increase your peak performance in line with your new personal best.

I will now take you through each of the elements of the SMART TRAINER guide and expand where appropriate. I will also share with you more detail on 'how' it is done so that you can begin using the technique or strategy at your next training event.

First of all, so that you don't have to keep flipping back to the front of the book, let's remind ourselves of the guide's elements:

Skilful	Trustworthy
Mastery	Resolve
Authority	Adroit
Ready	Innovative
Transfer	Navigator
	Energetic
	Rewarding

You will now be taken through each one of these in turn to ensure that the full meaning and implications are clearly understood. You will then begin to see just how you can put each of these into practice on a regular basis. In fact this guide will become your working template. If you are genuinely intent on becoming a SMART trainer then this guide will become your code of conduct.

Simple yet effective and powerful

All SMART trainers, even if they do it on a subconscious level, work to these guidelines. When I began my own route of self-development in order to achieve my goal of being the very best at my profession, I researched, observed and read my way through hundreds and hundreds of hours of material.

I discovered that attitudes and beliefs were central to the SMART trainer's high level of performance and success and you will be exploring them in the next chapter. I also discovered that there was a pattern of behaviours, the 'how tos' of making it happen as well. And this is how this code of conduct came about. Here I have formulated it, in true trainer fashion, into an acronym that aids its understanding and recall. It also adds a bit of fun to the whole process, and why not.

Most people enjoy success quite sporadically. They may have a great day, where all goes well and they deal with difficulties with relative ease. Yet, this can be followed by an awful day; they don't seem to be able to resolve the difficulties that they seemed to manage the day before. Why is this? People put it down to the general unpredictability of life. Sure, life can be pretty unpredictable; people can be fine one minute and moody the next. I found the possible reason for many of these incidents and once recognized I realized it could be better controlled.

Perform by default or design

The main thrust of all of my training events is to take the chance element out of people's lives by getting them to learn the appropriate skills and techniques so that they can combat the working day's problems by design rather than by default. Most people operate by default most of the time. On the days where they managed to successfully deal with a conflict issue, they did and said the right things that were needed at that moment and they got a result. However, they will not be aware of exactly what it was that they did or said. They got lucky and through the right combination of a variety of elements experienced a successful outcome. Learning to do this by design could prove rather beneficial.

So it is with any profession. All trainers that I come across will share with me experiences of great courses and not so great courses. Where the course has not been so successful it will always be put down to the group of people they were training or the training conditions that they had to work in. Of course these two elements have an impact, but they can be managed quite easily as long as you know how. And that is the key to fantastic training, to SMART training, giving people the know-how. I strongly encourage you to become a devotee to the SMART TRAINER code of conduct. It will make your job so much easier and enjoyable, it will enhance your effectiveness and increase your reputation as a true professional. Here is your route to SMART TRAINER know-how.

As you work your way through each of the elements of the SMART TRAINER acronym, make connections and trigger notes that will help you establish the key links with your Action Plan. This will make the end process of completing the final draft that much easier and quicker and you can begin working on it straight away.

THE SMART TRAINER CODE OF CONDUCT

Skilful

This is the art of developing yourself and the people you train. Obviously trainers must be skilful in training other people to become skilful. How skilful are you in your craft? How do you measure your skill? How much time do you allocate to your own development? When was the last time you attended a learning event for trainers?

If you find it difficult to answer these questions, or you have answered the last question along the lines that as a trainer of many years standing I don't need any trainer training, then **warning**! You have just lost a life as a SMART trainer.

SMART trainers never skimp on their own development and learning experiences, whether it is through reading books, listening to an audiotape in the car or attending seminars and workshops. My specialist subject is communication skills, particularly dealing with conflict and confrontation. I recently attended a seminar/workshop on 'Creative relationships'. While many of the inputs were known to me, it allowed me to revisit them from the viewpoint of another 'expert'. It also meant that I was hearing and thinking about the processes once more – and repetition is the master of skill. New pieces of information were covered too. All in all it was a very worthwhile exercise and it made a pleasant change to be a delegate. This also allowed me to observe the trainer's delivery techniques and to see if there was anything new to learn there too.

SMART trainers work hard at practising what they preach and pay attention to their own development needs. Begin by booking yourself on to a workshop on the subject you specialize in, read a training skills book or listen to an audiotape.

Mastery

This builds on the previous element. SMART trainers are not satisfied with just being skilful; they want to achieve *mastery* of their profession and specialist subject.

SMART trainers always have an air of control about them; they are in command – of the situation, of the training programme, of their subject. They have the upper hand in the training situation and use it with stealth.

After a short time on a SMART trainer's training course or workshop you realize that he or she is in possession of great knowledge and skill, displayed with confidence and charm. SMART trainers don't boast about it; it would be very easy and tempting to do so, but they resist because it would lose them the reputation of a SMART trainer. They are not insecure about their craft; they have nothing to prove, only great things to share.

The reason that SMART trainers are such avid readers is because they feel so passionate about their profession and craft that they want to absorb everything they can on their specialist subject, their own personal development and skill of training. They know that the more they learn and absorb, the greater will be their knowledge base.

Authority

This is not used in the usual sense of the word. Although most NIGHTMARE trainers behave with an air of superior authority, SMART trainers adopt the alternative definition of the word. They have learnt through their own development that to read up on a subject for three years will make them an expert, while to read up on it for five years will make them an authority on that subject.

It is through being both a master and an authority that SMART trainers can establish their credibility with their audiences very quickly. It is essential this is done so that delegates can relax and settle down into the learning that they are there to achieve as early in the training day as possible. Many delegates, if they doubt your credibility on the subject or your profession, will put up barriers and begin behaving in a way that is detrimental to good learning.

So, to briefly summarize the first three elements of the code: you need to determine the skill sets you need and at what level you currently operate. You will need to identify the skills, knowledge and techniques that you should develop further, in priority order, and then decide how best this can be achieved. Create a prioritized list of development/learning assignments and work through it over the coming year, through a combination of reading, listening to audiotapes and attending workshops or seminars.

Another option to consider is the use of a mentor. This would be someone whose work you have great respect and admiration for and whom you can meet up with on a regular basis. If meeting isn't that easy then consider telephone coaching as a means to achieve your development/learning assignments.

Ready

SMART trainers are a bit like boy scouts: they're always prepared. They work to a strict discipline when it comes to course preparation and being able to respond quickly to training requests.

They develop the habit of re-preparing their course material immediately after they have finished a particular course. We all know what happens if we fail to do this – when we come to prepare for the next course we discover just how much of a mess we left our materials in. And this usually happens when we don't have much time. It causes us much frustration and often leads to items being overlooked and forgotten.

Use your laminated checklist to re-sort and tidy the course material box, or whatever system you use, so that you relax, knowing that when that course comes round again, as it surely will, the preparation time will be greatly reduced and you are in control.

Transfer

If you're not transferring then it's not training, it's lecturing. Audiences generally hate being lectured at, but they love getting involved, being made to think through smart questions, having their current beliefs on how things work challenged.

SMART trainers ensure that their training event is designed and delivered so that it achieves true transfer of the key knowledge, skills, strategies and techniques that the delegates are there to receive.

And because SMART trainers are excited about the subject they teach, their audience enjoys having that excitement transferred to them too. The course energy levels increase, the learning becomes fun and the transferring of the key elements of the course becomes even easier.

This is all done by design with SMART trainers. This happens on every course that they run, which is why they keep on being asked to come back.

Trustworthy

One of the most important things for the trainer to establish very early on in the proceedings, besides personal credibility, is trust. Training-room confidentiality is crucial for a sound trainer/trainee relationship.

Trainers can win their delegates over far more easily and create a far superior learning atmosphere within the training room if they can really be allowed to open up. They are quite prepared to be very revealing about their situation at work if they feel safe in doing so.

I remember when I worked for a company as a training officer in my early days, being at a meeting to discuss a training programme with my boss and a number of directors. We had got to the point where we were discussing the reasons why some areas of the business were better at getting their people attending the courses than others. During the previous courses I had run, through the promise of confidentiality, I had received some very useful feedback that deserved to be followed up in order to establish its accuracy and then to decide how best to deal with it. I gave my feedback, which was to do with the way some of the department's managers viewed training and their commitment to it.

The director who was in charge of this area asked who had given me the information. I asked why he needed to know; after all, the main point was that this had been flagged up, no one was making any accusations, but at least we could take a closer look and find out for ourselves. He became quite agitated when I wouldn't give him names, at first saying that no one was going to get into trouble, but that it would help him if he knew who had given the feedback.

I refused to divulge my source for two reasons. First, because it had no bearing on the issue that needed exploring and secondly, I knew that even if the person didn't get in to trouble he would know, and so would others, how their confidential feedback had become public. To have done anything different would have damaged not only the confidentiality factor of all future courses, but my reputation and credibility as well. This would be far too high a price to pay.

Even today, as an independent consultant, when I am asked to feedback any potential problem issues that may be harboured by the delegates I always refuse to identify contributors and I explain to the client exactly why. I always ensure that I back this up with the fact that the information is the real focus, not the person delivering it, and stress that the client wants to create a workforce that is pro-training. They always agree.

Resolve

While all SMART trainers are resolved to make every learning experience fun and worthwhile for everyone, they also display great resolve when it is required.

We do not train in a perfect world. Ah! If only. If there is one thing that people hate more than anything else, it's a whiner. Particularly the whiners who rumble into action as soon as the smallest element of the training experience is not quite right.

Sometimes you have to do your very best with less than the best in terms of equipment, room set-up, size and ventilation, hotel or conference centre service.

SMART trainers have a fixity of purpose that means they will always treat the transferring of the key skills to their delegates as paramount, and sometimes that means improvising or adapting your usual style. In other words, sometimes you just have to make do with what you've got and get on and do it to the same high SMART trainer standards.

I once had to deliver a training course for new starters in what seemed like a broom cupboard. Normally the delegates would attend the training centre but, due to abnormally high labour turnover, in one particular depot there were 14 people who all needed to learn how to complete the appropriate bookwork and systems information in order to do the jobs they had been employed for.

The branch manager asked whether, rather than disrupt their on-job training, I could come in and take them through a series of half-day workshops at the depot. I was told that they had an appropriate room that would hold the 14 delegates, no problem. 'No problem' turned out to be an untruth. The room was the manager's office, which was right next to the main product storage rooms, which were in constant use with loading and unloading. The room was about 12 foot by 10 foot. They had moved tables in from the restroom and placed them classroom-style across the room so that once I was positioned at the front I was stuck there until they all left the room.

The workshop had to be run with an overhead projector. I set up the travel projector in the only place I was able, propped on top of its case between two desks with a delegate sat either side. This looked decidedly dodgy as it wobbled precariously every time someone fidgeted. The guy nearest the projector was a permanent fidget, whom I warned on many occasions to beware of the projector. It was all to no avail: when my back was turned he fidgeted some more and brought the whole thing crashing down.

That particular course really did test my resolve. I put it down to experience but kept my focus on the job in hand – to get the delegates fully trained in the best way and with the most fun. It was challenging and fun and everybody had a laugh, especially at the projector incident.

So, an attitude of adaptability and flexibility is an essential SMART trainer trait, which is then added to by the next element.

Adroit

SMART trainers have shrewdness about them. They are extremely observant and assess the situation that they find themselves in very quickly. They assess the training room immediately on arrival and evaluate how the workshop proceedings will roll out within such confines.

There will always be difficulties and SMART trainers exercise resourcefulness and readiness to change course at an instant if the situation calls for it. This allows them to take these situations in their stride, because they know how essential it is to remain focused on the wellbeing of the delegate.

Innovative

Get into the habit of always searching for new approaches and different routes to the same destination. There are many roads that lead to Rome, but if you keep on taking the same one every time you travel there it will become boring.

Familiarity breeds contempt and this is no less true when delivering training courses and workshops. Train yourself to become innovative and inventive. Explore new ways of delivering the same topics. Look for new activities, new case studies, and new ways of explaining. Sure, it will take more time initially, but it will be worth the investment in time and effort. It will keep you fresh and on top form and focused on delivering the very best to your delegates every time you train. That's why SMART trainers are smart.

Navigator

SMART trainers learn the art of being able to navigate their delegates through the learning journey via the easiest route for recall and understanding. This doesn't mean that the training isn't both challenging and fun. It does mean that all learning sessions are interlinked both forward to the road ahead where the delegates are yet to go, and back to where they have come from. This enables the delegates to recognize points along the journey and to be able to retrace their steps in order to aid recall and to 'see' how it all fits together.

The SMART trainer sees the learning event as a huge jigsaw of knowledge, skills, strategies, techniques and tactics that need piecing together. The delegates get given the pieces to put together while the SMART trainer acts as the picture on the lid that keeps them encouraged enough to keep on working on the pieces until they are placed together correctly.

The methods employed to produce this effect are given in detail in Chapter 12, where you get the opportunity to put them into action on the next course you run.

Energetic

Nobody likes monotone voices or static displays. The energy levels of all training events run by the SMART trainer are never left to chance. This is because they know just how critical the right energy levels within the training environment are to the success of the whole event.

SMART trainers learn how to control the pace of the course and the energy levels that reside within the delegates at any given time. They teach themselves what to look out for, what signs they need to be aware of which indicate that a change of pace is required. To ignore these signs is to consign the training course to TRADITIONAL training methods at best, NIGHTMARE training methods at worst.

SMART trainers are aware of the impact their delivery is having on the energy of the group at any given time and they adjust the process accordingly. They may insert an additional mini-group exercise, like a buzz group if energy levels start flagging. This works particularly well if the room is not very good. They may also change tactics and change a group or paired exercise to an individual one if they feel that the energy level is getting too high for focused learning.

Make sure you are fully trained in the art of group dynamics and how to manipulate the energy within the group and this will move you one step closer to the status you desire.

Rewarding

Reward is the key motivator of the training experience. We all enjoy rewards and SMART trainers make sure that everybody is very clear as to what the rewards will be right at the outset of the training event. They ensure that everyone knows what the reward will feel, look and smell like.

I will always begin my courses with a little negotiation with the delegates on the course timings; this establishes whether anyone has any other plans that they haven't told me about. This begins the relationship-building process and tells them that the course is theirs. We strike a deal: if anyone needs to go before the course is programmed to end, we achieve all of the tasks (I want their commitment to keep focused, on time and in here). We then establish a revised finish time that everyone agrees to.

The SMART trainer then moves on to spell out the benefits of attending the programme and what they can do to increase those benefits even further. The delegates look forward to the planned sessions and the trainers enjoy the whole process much more because of the willingness of the delegates to throw themselves into the learning. It's called 'everybody wins'.

Now you're ready to move on to the next chapter of the programme where you can explore the philosophies, attitudes and behaviours of the SMART trainer in more depth.

The SMART trainer's summary of Chapter 9

In summary, you covered, learnt and worked on the following key factors that will help you achieve Beyond Traditional Training status by investing in your own development and becoming a SMART trainer:

- took the first step on how to become a SMART trainer;
- learnt the SMART trainer's code of conduct;
- discovered ways of putting the code into practice for yourself;
- learnt the detail of each element of the code;
- visualized carrying out each element of the code.

10

THE SMART TRAINER'S PHILOSOPHY AND PROFESSIONAL ATTITUDE

'Your philosophy will determine whether you will go for the disciplines or continue the errors.'

(Jim Rohn)

Your learning objectives in this chapter

By the end of this chapter you will have:

- learnt how to develop a professional attitude and mindset that guarantees SMART trainer status and success;
- discovered the philosophies of the SMART trainer in order to develop your own;
- developed a philosophy that you can work to for personal satisfaction and self-improvement.

I suppose the first question to ask is, 'Do you really want to become a SMART trainer?' I believe that if you have read this far into the book then the answer must be an emphatic 'yes'. If that is true then the fact that you are putting the effort in to complete the programme is a typical SMART trainer behaviour – although like all SMART trainers I don't like to make assumptions or take things for granted.

And that is one of the first things to be clear about: if your aim is to become a SMART trainer then it isn't just a set of rules that you follow at certain times of the day or week. It is a way of life. It is the code of conduct you have just gone through. It is a certain mindset. Now the philosophy and attitudes of SMART trainers will be covered in detail as you work through this chapter but before you can work on those two very important elements you must have the right mindset installed. What is your mindset?

WORKING TO A POSITIVE MINDSET

In order to become a SMART trainer you have to be delivering training in a certain style, a style that is far removed from training in the traditional sense of the word. The style is a behaviour, or the way in which things are done in relation to transferring knowledge, skills, strategies, techniques and tactics to trainees or delegates. The key word here, as you will now be very much aware, is 'transferring'.

Whether you are transferring or not will depend on how your training course has been designed and the principles and strategies you adopt and put into practice while carrying out that design and subsequent delivery. I will take you through the key principles that SMART trainers work to later on in the chapter; for now though let's explore mindsets a little more.

We often get delegates who have been sent to courses who seriously believe that they cannot learn anything. They use the age-old excuse that they are too old or not bright enough (and I have had people on courses as young as their mid-30s who believe this to be true for them). When speaking to these people you can see that they are telling you the truth; they really believe what they are saying. It is their mindset.[1]

This negative mindset is often further entrenched by their experience on the training course that they have been made to attend. For instance, someone who truly believes that they are too old to learn anything new attends a training course. This person is confronted with a TRADITIONAL trainer (or worse still a NIGHTMARE trainer) who, due to his or her training methods, fails to transfer or build enough confidence into the delegate (or if it's a NIGHTMARE trainer, further undermines the delegate's confidence). As a direct result, the delegate will fail to learn anything new and will put this down as confirmation that he or she is 'too old', or 'not clever enough' and give him or herself a pat on the back for being right.

Note that negative people are always right. They don't expect to do well so they don't put as much effort or concentration into it and therefore set themselves up to fail, which in turn proves that they were right. This act of being right then becomes their focus, because being right feels good to them and they want to keep repeating this false 'feel-good' factor. And because of this misdirected focus they fail to realize that they are praising themselves for failing. It becomes a vicious cycle that they find hard to break free from.

The story of a self-fulfilling prophecy in action

I'm reminded of the story of the small café owner, who was enthusiastic but a little gullible and susceptible to other people's interference due to his mindset created by his lack of self-belief and confidence. His premises were slightly off the beaten track but, because he had taken the advice of a successful fellow businessman and advertised widely, and due to the fact that he delivered a great service and fantastic food, he did well. That is, until one day a negative self-confessed expert happened upon his café in response to the barrage of advertisements he had come across in all the local publications. The café was full but it was only a short wait until he got served.

He told the café owner that he was surprised to see so many advertisements placed in all the various publications and that it must be costing him a small fortune. The café owner agreed that it wasn't cheap, but that he believed that it brought in trade that he wouldn't otherwise have had.

The businessman said that he wondered why the café owner thought he needed so much advertising, as he looked around the crowded tables; the café was obviously very popular. The self-confessed expert then added, 'Don't you realize that there is a recession on, companies are going bust all over the place? You have to tighten your belt during such times, it's not wise to spend so much money on advertising during a recession when there are less people who are able to respond to your adverts anyway.'

This got the café owner thinking that maybe he was being a little extravagant, given the recession. So he decided to reduce his advertising by half for a while and monitor how things went.

Three months later the negative self-confessed expert popped into the café again. This time he had no wait to get served as the café was less than half full. The café owner recognized the self-confessed expert and thanked him for his advice on saving some money by reducing his advertising budget. 'You were right,' he said, 'that recession is really starting to hit now. Thank goodness I'm spending less on my advertising.'

Beware the power of the self-fulfilling prophecy

That little fable is actually acted out by many companies, both large and small, every time the economy hits a rough patch. They listen to the doom and gloom merchants and don't want to take the risk of following their own path. Mindsets are powerful things, and that applies to both the positive and negative types.

We can all very easily create our own self-fulfilling prophecies, so we must be careful in what we create. Remember: whatever it is that you do create through your mindset and subsequent actions you will have to live with. Make sure the results are ones you'll enjoy living with and not end up regretting.

Self-fulfilling prophecies are where this programme is taking you. By the end of this book you will have designed a powerful set of personal goals and strategies that when put into action will create your desired outcomes.

SMART trainers always see the class half-full

How easy is it to change attitude? The answer, as anyone who has ever tried will tell you, is not very. And recognizing this in yourself is crucial to making those necessary behaviour changes that will separate you from the TRADITIONAL trainer. Attitude is just your thinking habits, repeated every day. It is the way you currently see things because at sometime in the past you chose to see and believe something in a certain way and acted accordingly. Eventually this became a Stage 4 of learning and before you knew it you were doing it without knowing. Operating on autopilot.

As it is your attitude that drives your behaviours, then you know that the resistance you will surely encounter in making the transition will be of your own making. This is due to the discomfort caused by interfering with the autopilot mechanism within us. This realization is great news, for if you know why you are resisting any behaviour change then you can control the process and make necessary compensations while you create new habits of thinking.

Your point of view is coloured by the way you feel, which in turn is affected by your attitude towards what you're seeing. If 5 of your 10 delegates fail to turn up, do you see a half-empty or half-full classroom? Do you say, 'Damn, only half turned up' or, 'Great, at least we had half turn up; these are the lucky ones that I will be able to help.'

ATTITUDES, BEHAVIOURS AND THE LAW OF CAUSE AND EFFECT

We can also tie this in with the universal law of cause and effect, particularly in the form of 'behaviour breeds behaviour'. For instance, if you are feeling particularly negative about a training event then the behaviours you display, including the tone and pace of your speech, will reflect this. In turn your audience will be receiving these messages, some so subtle that they will be unaware of them on a conscious level, but they will begin to be influenced by them none the less. Their attitude towards the event and you will generate a form of behaviour that you will pick up on, through both the conscious and subconscious levels, and this will feed your attitude and behaviour. And so the negative cycle flows ever downward.

How you feel is what we get

I always remind my delegates to be aware of their attitude when dealing with other people, for they can never hide or disguise it. No matter how good you believe you are at hiding your internal thoughts and feelings about something, believe me, you are as transparent as a freshly polished pane of crystal glass. So, you feel it and we get it.

And because our attitudes are habits of thought we must train ourselves out of the bad habits and into the good and most appropriate ones. You must change your behaviours first, retrain the physical methods you operate by. This is how you change attitude – through the associated behaviour. If you want to change the destination then you have to change the route. If you keep on arriving at the same poor result then take a look at the behaviours you exercised to get there and you will find what you have to work on to put things right. You can do this quite easily if you follow the simple steps I will now share with you.

CHANGING YOUR NEGATIVE THINKING HABITS

When we think negative we are talking ourselves out of something, talking ourselves down and away from the actual desired outcomes that we want. Remember, before every action there is a thought, whether that thought is conscious or subconscious.

Now that you are on the threshold of becoming a SMART trainer your awareness will be raised and you will start noticing a great deal more detail in your day-to-day activities and your life in general. This means that even thoughts that were previously on your subconscious level will become noticeable to you.

The great thing about the SMART trainer code of conduct and the skills that you learn and put into practice is that they generate results in all areas of your life, not just work. So working on this crucial area of behaviour and attitude change has double benefits.

The four-step process

Whenever you find yourself in the position of thinking negative then you must take immediate action. Here are the steps I recommend you follow.

Step 1

Catch yourself making the thought and stop. Raise your awareness to the actual situation you are in.

Step 2

Hold the thought in your mind for a moment in order to retake control of your thought process. In other words, move it back into the workings of the conscious mind and out of the clutches of the subconscious.

Step 3

Challenge the thought. Debate with yourself about how you can justify doing the opposite of what your original thought was telling you to do.

For every reason that you come up with for not doing something, or doing it in the more cautious or negative way, match it with a positive reason and benefit for doing it.

Step 4

Flip the thought over and act on the opposite side of your original negative thought. So, if your original thought was that you believed that (whatever it is) couldn't be done at all, or couldn't be done 'that' way, you will now believe that it can be done. So what action will you now take to achieve that positive outcome and enjoy the benefits of the positive action?

While this appears overly simple at first sight it is extremely effective, and remember it is the simple systems that usually are the most powerful and productive. This easy-to-practise process will help you to change any habit that you currently have that is holding you back.

The 21-day rule

My delegates are always amazed when I tell them how long it will take them to change bad habits (behaviours that hold them back from their desired outcomes) to good habits (behaviours that move them towards their desired outcomes). And this is what you will have to do if you want to achieve that SMART trainer status. The beauty of this is that it is really easy and in the scheme of our lives produces results very quickly.

Whenever I ask people how long they believe it takes to make or break a habit (a great way to check their current beliefs and attitudes) they usually answer along the lines of: 'Depends how long you've been doing the thing you want to change' or, 'Depends what the habit is'. The reality is that it depends on neither of those two.

People have said that it must take years, or at the best many months. This a natural assumption to make because they are comparing the changing of the habit, which is no more than a repeated behaviour, with the length of time they have been doing it. There is no connection to this; the connection is with something you can very easily control.

The habit-changing process is connected to the way we learn and we can relate this to the four stages of learning. (If you need to you can recap on the four stages of learning by going back to Chapter 4.) While we are still between Stages 2 and 3 we are consciously carrying out the new skills, initially under some tuition and supervision. Once we have mastered it we keep repeating it over and over again until eventually the conscious process is not needed anymore as we move into Stage 4, the level of unconscious competence. Our good friend 'autopilot' kicks in and takes over; this is also known as 'habit'.

You now have the answer to breaking or changing a habit. We consistently repeat the new process again and again until it replaces the old process. Research shows that on average this takes about 21 days. That's right, just 21 days, but it has to be 21 days of continuous practice of the 'new' behaviour that you want to ingrain into your subconscious for the 'autopilot' process to take over. This is more difficult when associated with certain behaviours, such as smoking or any other kind of drug intake, as the body has to deal with the extra element of addiction.

If you break the process before the 21 days has been reached you will need to restart from the beginning. You will be getting plenty of practice in this great little technique when you begin your Action Plan, but I recommend that you give it a test drive on something you would like to change. Start tonight. Try something relatively simple to start with, maybe something quite frivolous. It's only to prove to yourself that it really does work.

The example I use on my workshops is getting dressed. As a man I use a male dressing example. Which sock do I put on first when getting dressed in the morning? As I am right-handed I always put my left sock on first; this is a habit that I have followed for well over 35 years now. If I wanted to change this to putting my right sock on first, then from now on I would have to make a conscious effort to break the left-foot habit and create the right-foot habit.

Now if this was something that I felt so strongly about that I was determined to succeed then I would organize myself to be more consciously aware at the appropriate times. I would put a variety of reminders in place that ensured I followed my new dressing procedures for the next 21 days. At the end of that period, if I had acted on all of my reminders at every appropriate opportunity, I would be putting my right sock on first without even consciously thinking about it.

You will be adopting this method of habit breaking and making for the successful achievement of your Action Plan.

Now we will re-visit the philosophy of the SMART trainer so that you can determine one of your own, which will enable you to discover and act with the ultimate professional attitude that will bring you SMART trainer status and success.

THE PHILOSOPHY AND ULTIMATE PROFESSIONAL ATTITUDE OF THE SMART TRAINER

The philosophy

You must have a sound philosophy, a primary aim to focus on and travel towards. As a trainer who commands great respect from your peers and participants on all of your training events, and as a trainer who earns what you are really worth, you must be crystal clear about this point.

Establishing your philosophy is important as it creates the energy that drives you on to achieve the goals you have set yourself. It also works in harmony with the power of the universal laws that govern what we receive in our lives. We have all seen the power of these through the examples in Chapter 8 and in our own life, with the most common experience being the law of cause and effect, or sowing and reaping.

Let me share with you again my philosophy as an example. My philosophy of life is really very simple. I want to do great things for others and I want great things for myself. I truly believe that 'Your success is my success' is a philosophy worth working towards. And it has all the hallmarks of greatness, power and the ability to work and produce the results I want. It's short, simple and straight to the point. It contains just five words yet those five words conjure up a very vivid and powerful image for me.

I am showing you this again as an example of what your philosophy could be. It is always much easier to produce something once you have seen what it should look and sound like. So, produce a philosophy statement for yourself now.

The great thing with philosophies is that even when they are identical to someone else's they still remain unique to the individual. This is because they will never be identical in the personal motives and emotions that created it. For instance, the images and emotions that are created within me when I repeat the five words of my philosophy are what I associate with and are what I see as happening in my life as a consequence of putting my philosophy into action on a daily basis. Of course the images and emotions that you would associate with the same five words would be as a direct consequence of your own current circumstances.

So please feel free to use the same five words as I have. You will not be copying, it will not be cheating, and the philosophy will still be yours. The important thing here is to have a philosophy that you can take ownership of and begin living by, for this is the very nucleus of the SMART trainer's positive impact on others through excellent training delivery. If you like it is the starter motor for all your future actions and their consequences. Write in the philosophy you will live and work by in the box below.

You can refer back to this when producing your Action Plan in Chapter 12.

The professional attitude

All SMART trainers possess and work to a professional attitude. The way they think, talk and act is highly professional at all times. They remain objective, even in the most emotional of circumstances. They remain focused on their primary aim and purpose of being. They have their philosophy to guide and drive them and their behaviour towards delegates and client/boss alike is shaped by the attitude of the true professional.

So, what is meant by a 'professional attitude'? What is your understanding of the term 'professional'? When we say that someone was so professional, what exactly do we mean? How do you identify professionalism?

As the SMART trainer is a true professional you need to establish the key criteria if you are to emulate this. I have seen people spend huge amounts of time debating this subject and coming up with reams of 'key elements' that go to make someone truly professional. This is unnecessary because there really is only one element of true professionalism. And once you have uncovered what that one element is, and most people are surprised by how simple and ordinary it is, then you can begin practising the art of true professionalism.

Who cares?

The true professional, that's who. If you break down all the component parts that go to make up a professional, in its truest form, it always comes back to the same act. The act of caring. Look at this explanation of the true professional:

- They care for their profession.
- They care for the company they work for.
- They care for their product.
- They care for the service they give.
- They care for the client, delegate or customer.
- They care for themselves.
- They care about continuously improving themselves.
- They care about the people who work for them.
- They care about the people who work with them.
- They care about the quality of their work.
- They care about the impression they communicate to others.

If you genuinely care for all of those elements then your whole demeanour and actions will automatically flow positively and productively. The universal law of sowing and reaping kicks in big time.

Anyone who does not subscribe to and work at each of these elements with commitment is not a true professional. There is no such thing as a part-time professional. I have come across many company trainers, managers and independent consultants who sell themselves as professionals in their field, who then reveal through conversation an attitude that conflicts with the professional care code. The most common element missed out is the one on continuous self-improvement. I'm sorry, but all of these elements are mandatory if they are to have the desired effect that the true professional strives to achieve. You are allowed to fail, but you are not allowed not to try.

MAKING PEOPLE WANT TO LEARN

Learning is a voluntary act. So how do you get people to want to learn? SMART trainers find motivating people to learn comes naturally because they are operating to the true professional dictum. If you really believe in the rules of true professionalism then that will come through loud and clear in your whole approach to the task in hand.

It will affect the way you think the process through, the way you design the programme, the way you prepare for the course and the way you deliver it. It influences the words you use, the body language you display and the questions you ask.

For instance, delegates will only be willing to try out new techniques and learn new ways of working if they really believe that the trainer is interested, cares and genuinely wants to help them work better and easier.

I always open my courses by telling my audience that my job responsibilities are to make their jobs easier and more fun. I then ask the great 'yes' question: 'Would you like to be able to do your job easier than you do it now and have more fun doing it?' Everyone either nods or says yes. This is a great technique for getting people to change their viewpoint away from the negative, 'This course is a waste of time I'd would rather be back at work in my comfort zone' and on to something that they can picture as a possible benefit to them.

I then go on to tell them that I know that they already work hard in their job, a safe assumption as everybody believes this of themselves, and it gives them a quick burst of recognition that generates a feel-good factor. I then continue by saying that by the end of this course they will also be able to work smarter in their job. I then ask another 'yes' question: 'Would you be interested in learning how you could work smarter in your job?' Again, I receive maximum agreement to this.

By establishing this at the very beginning of the programme I set the scene for the training events ahead and create an element of curiosity that will keep the sceptical delegate interested long enough to get involved in the whole learning experience. And because I care about the benefits they will receive from taking part in the workshop, I will work hard at making this happen in the most fun way possible.

BUILDING ON SOLID FOUNDATIONS

You have now reached the point where you can progress on to the next chapter and begin to establish the key actions that SMART trainers carry out. You will see how SMART trainers present themselves in a variety of situations. Let's summarize the key points of this chapter and then move on.

The SMART trainer's summary of Chapter 10

In summary, you covered, learnt and worked on the following key factors that will help you achieve Beyond Traditional Training status by investing in your own development and becoming a SMART trainer. You:

- discovered the pitfalls of working to an incorrect mindset;
- learnt the power of the self-fulfilling prophecy;
- learnt the true power of attitude;
- discovered that you must change behaviour in order to correct attitude;
- looked at the link between attitude, behaviour and the law of cause and effect;
- learnt the steps needed to change negative thinking habits;
- learnt the four-step process;
- were introduced to the 21-day rule;
- created your own unique philosophy;
- discovered the professional attitude;
- explored a technique to get people to want to learn;
- learnt that the SMART trainer is a true professional who cares.

Note

1. Link back to Chapter 2 for other examples of faulty mindsets.

11

HOW SMART TRAINERS PRESENT THEMSELVES

'The Bible gives us a list of human stories on both sides of the ledger. One list of human stories is used as examples – do what these people did. Another list of human stories is used as warnings – don't do what these people did. So if your story ever gets in one of these books, make sure they use it as an example, not a warning.'

(Jim Rohn)

Your learning objectives in this chapter

By the end of this chapter you will have:

- observed through case-study examples and real-life anecdotes how SMART trainers compare to TRADITIONAL trainers when presenting themselves within the training profession;
- learnt how SMART trainers dress to impress on audiences their credibility and professionalism.

A CRITICAL PIECE OF THE JIGSAW

If we return to the jigsaw analogy that we used earlier in your programme, and compare all of the attributes of the SMART trainer with five pieces of a jigsaw, then you will see how they all fit together. With each of the five pieces representing the top-level headings of knowledge, skill, techniques and strategy, with image and personal presentation as the central piece, then you will appreciate why 'image' is so critical. Its position is always central to everything. (Look at Figure 11.1 to see what I mean.) This is due to the influences that this particular piece delivers on its own and through the other four areas as they are brought into play by the trainer. It is critical that you realize that it is one of the central pieces that all the other pieces connect to and therefore dictates how effective your training input really is. You may be the expert of all experts on the subject in hand but if I don't like you then I am not going to listen to you, let alone learn anything new. All information that is present in the other four pieces is channelled through that central piece. If this piece is missing then not only do you fail to complete the jigsaw, but you also fail to generate the necessary connections with other essential areas of the SMART trainer's attributes and skills.

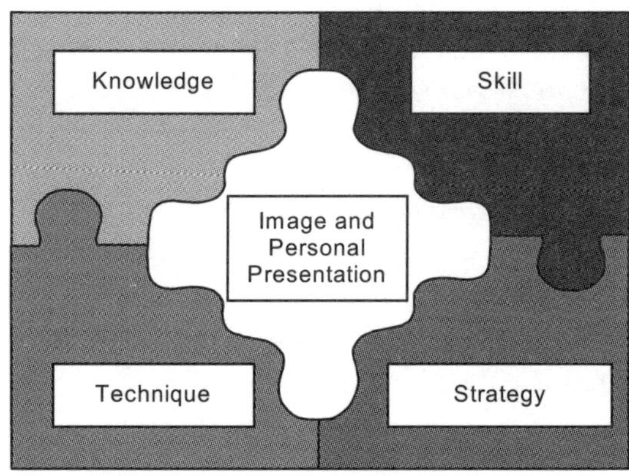

Figure 11.1 *The attributes jigsaw*

As you can see from Figure 11.1, with the central piece either missing or not being utilized in the right manner or with the right methods, a breakdown or blockage will occur when trying to pull on all other areas. When performing as a SMART trainer you must be drawing on all of the five regions in turn, and at times simultaneously. With a missing or damaged link within this framework, performance is affected and impact drops dramatically.

To give you another, more vivid example, you can see where both TRADITIONAL and NIGHTMARE trainers hit problems that they, or rather their delegates and people they do business with, encounter.

Both TRADITIONAL and NIGHTMARE trainers will have all of these pieces of the jigsaw in their makeup too. Let's assume that they have as good as, if not better, sources of information on knowledge, skill, technique and strategy, but because they are coming over as either a TRADITIONAL or NIGHTMARE trainer the problem most definitely lies in that central piece, 'image and personal presentation'.

Part of that central piece of 'image and personal presentation' is where we keep our personal traits, how we communicate with others, whether or not we build rapport with our audience or people we meet, our attitudes, beliefs, values and philosophy. If this area is either ignored or we fail to put its contents into practice correctly, then we have already seen what happens.

With TRADITIONAL and NIGHTMARE trainers most if not all of the jigsaw pieces are in need of attention to some detail. Whether it is keeping up to date with the latest thinking in the 'knowledge' piece, or learning new methods of delivery in the 'skills' piece, from my experience it is usually a combination of areas and items that are lacking.

If we take NIGHTMARE trainers as an example, their central jigsaw piece will be encrypted with their own perceived image of themselves. Many NIGHTMARE trainers suffer from delusions of grandeur and a superiority complex. This affects the way they are perceived by the people they are paid to influence. They come across with an air of pomposity, or they come over in a patronizing manner – whichever it is, the result is often the same: the audience will buy nothing this person tries to sell them.

Keeping your jigsaw intact

As so many of the skills and attributes are interlinking, to have a major piece that acts as a crucial conduit disconnected or infected with an egotistical flaw will shut down many of the key areas required for you to operate as a SMART trainer. You will then fail to operate at the truly professional level that is expected of all SMART trainers and will not receive all the rewards and benefits that SMART trainers enjoy.

Judging a book by its cover and other such aphorisms

Whenever I cover this on any of my workshops someone usually says, 'But that's not right, you should not judge people by the way they look.'

I agree with them because you shouldn't. I say, 'You're absolutely right, people shouldn't judge others on the way they look, but I'll give you a clue… they do. We all do, even you.'

Sure, once someone gets to know you better they will discover what an honest, bright, warm person you are, but before they do that they're going to take a good look. And everybody does this; it's human nature. We have a look, take what we see and compare it with our current library of similar images and make a judgement based on the information that this gives us. We're doing this all of the time. Looking, processing, judging and then taking the necessary actions that harmonize with that judgement. It's an internal safety mechanism that tries to stop us walking into problems. Admittedly we get it wrong a lot of the time but that's because we haven't yet mastered the art of suspending our initial judgement while we explore for more information to give us a more accurate and clearer picture.

It is part and parcel of this existence we call life. It has always happened and it always will, so don't waste valuable time and energy in trying to change what is written deep into everyone's DNA. The easiest and far more effective route is to stop doing it with others and learn how to deal with it to reduce its effects on you. Learn the preventative measures you need to take, build them into your strategy for personal achievement and success and then action it. That's something for you to do in Chapter 12 when you produce your Action Plan.

If you want business advice, ask the gardener!

As image and personal presentation are the bedrock of achieving SMART trainer status, before moving on to explore how exactly SMART trainers present themselves so that you can check your own presentation, we will quickly look at a couple of fun examples.

Imagine that you have decided to start your own business. Who would you go to for financial advice? Well, there would be your bank manager, an accountant (preferably recommended to you by someone you could trust) and an independent financial adviser. All seem fair enough to me.

Why not go to the local garden centre owner instead? I mean they would know quite a bit about business finances, could even know more than the so-called experts. They'd almost definitely know more about running a small business than your average rookie bank manager. We won't risk it, but what is it that we are really risking? Why do we choose to go to the obvious so-called experts? We go because of the perception, the image, we hold of them and this has been conditioned into us since birth.

Another example would be the following scenario: you walk into your bank manager's office for your small business appointment and discover him sat there dressed like a gardener ready to begin the muck spreading.[1] How do you react? Would he instil confidence in you? No? But why ever not? He's still the same person with all the same quality of financial advice. He forgot to put on his business suit today; big deal.

Of course it *is* a big deal. It causes us problems because it clashes with our preconceived idea of what we expect. Now let's explore this with trainers and their delegates or clients.

ESTABLISHING YOUR CREDIBILITY

If you want to establish your credibility with your audience, how is it best achieved? Your credibility is very precious to you; it is your passport to getting buy-in from your delegates as well as entry into many lucrative areas. You have to get it right and prove it as early as possible in the proceedings. Your audience will not begin to take you seriously until they are convinced that you are what you are presenting yourself to be.

I remember, some years back now, co-facilitating a group and introducing myself in the following way: 'My name is Ken Marshall and I've been in training for five years.' As I spoke these words the comic thought popped into my head that it made me sound like a very slow learner. I imagined them saying to themselves, 'Five years and still in training? I wonder if he'll ever graduate.' I didn't feel 100 per cent confident that I would have helped establish my credibility if they had taken that interpretation literally.

Credibility is really about empathy. The SMART trainer knows this and uses the skills and strategies that are stored in that central jigsaw piece to put over to the audience all of the key aspects of the other four pieces, in a way they will believe.

Now this may sound like you're trying to dupe your audience into believing something that isn't true. This is not what I mean at all. Let me tell you here and now: conning your audience that you're something you're not cannot be done. If it isn't true, you won't come across with sincerity and everybody I have ever met, from the humble shop floor cleaner to the highest executive, has an inbuilt insincerity detector, which is often referred to by another name that I will not repeat here. You will never get away with feeding people information about yourself, your experience and your background, that must connect you with them, their situation and their need for its improvement, if you and it do not add up.

Credibility is established when you recognize the situation your delegates are currently experiencing. You convince them that you have been there and that you can fully appreciate what they are going through, and that you have learnt over the years just how to deal with it successfully and will now share with them and show them during your time together how to do it better, easier, smarter, etc, so that they can improve it for themselves.

This is essential, whether it is to a group that you are training, or whether you are meeting a senior manager to talk about a new development programme. It also applies even if you're an independent consultant, seeing a prospective client. And once you have begun the process of establishing your credibility you then move up a gear and continue to build on it.

HOW TO CONDUCT YOUR AUDIENCE LIKE AN ORCHESTRA

Do you conduct yourself with panache and flair, or solemnity? What style of delivery would you prefer a trainer whose course you were attending to use? I know what I would prefer and my guess is so would about 99.9 per cent of all training course audiences.[2] I want to be shaken awake with the prospect of learning something new and encouraged to enjoy myself along the way. I want to be taught by a trainer who really has my best interests at heart and is eager to help me achieve my new skills. I want, no I demand, to be trained by someone who is passionate about his or her subject and who really believe in what they are saying.

So how do you conduct your training courses? Take a good look at your delegates the next time you are delivering a training session. How are they sitting? What is the expression on their faces? What do you see in their eyes?

Style versus content

If you are being interesting, your words delivered with energy, your enthusiasm almost tangible, then the chances are your audience will be leaning forward. The expression on their faces should have them looking engrossed and not embalmed. Their eyes should be on you most of the time as they follow your every word, with a look of intrigue and delight in them. Do you recognize any of this? If so, well done and keep it up. If not, then you have some work to do. This is no problem as all of this can be learnt with a little self-awareness, practice and patience. Remember, nobody is born a SMART trainer, everyone that exists had to learn his or her craft.

So many trainers deliver their material as if they have already decided that no one will enjoy it so they may as well accept the inevitable. The inevitable being, 'This material will bore them rigid because it bores me, so I may as well bore them as painlessly as possible.' Unfortunately this strategy never works because being bored by someone you feel should know how to avoid boring people makes the whole process depressing as well as boring. This is a recipe for disaster.

I will share with you a training experience that I had to endure when I worked as a training and recruitment manager for a large blue chip company. It has been indelibly etched into my brain forever. One day it was decided to insert a 45-minute training session on key subjects and issues into all of the human resource department's monthly meetings. As the meeting normally ran for the best part of a day this wouldn't prove too difficult to achieve and should make the meetings more interesting and productive. Well, while the theory was fine the practice turned out somewhat differently.

The very first one I had to endure, and I use the word 'endure' advisedly, was on the subject of health and safety. Now, before we go any further, the subject of health and safety is seen by many as one of those 'dry as old bones' kind of subjects. SMART trainers know, however, that there is no such thing as a dry subject, only dry trainers. Or dry people masquerading as trainers, as in this case. The session began with a confused and conflicting flurry of talk, which left everybody bewildered as to what the session was actually going to be about. So, no clarity of purpose, no objectives and no structure. That is he talked at us, his audience, as if we had the IQ of our shoe size and the common sense of a Member of Parliament on a freebie weekend away from home surrounded by the press. And from there on in it got progressively worse.

This became the longest 45 minutes of my life, and I would imagine everyone else's too, although to be fair I didn't seek their opinions. It then entered into a new level of brain-numbing boredom and patience-challenging effrontery, when overhead slides were beamed on to the screen resembling exact copies of text taken from the pages of *War and Peace*. This was then made worse (and you didn't think it was possible) by the trainer telling us, in a very paternal tone, to read it. He then, after a slight pause, proceeded to read it out to us, which was his way of saying, 'I don't believe that you'll read it'. There were 15 such slides. After just two I began to lose the will to live.

My colleague, sitting next to me, lent across and whispered that we should have filmed this so we could show it on our 'Train the Trainer' workshops as an example of how not to do it. As the sound of a police siren filtered into the room from somewhere down in the streets below, I lent across to my colleague in return and whispered, 'It's OK, the "bad trainer" police are on their way.' We entertained ourselves in this juvenile manner for the rest of his training session, in just the same way that any delegate would have done who had to suffer such a distressing excuse of a learning event. NIGHTMARE trainers be warned: I am out to expose and disband you.

That anecdote is one example of how not to communicate. To ensure you avoid anything like this, just do the opposite of everything he did. Let's now move on to another form of SMART trainer communication.

Style will always outscore content every time on the scale for measuring the impact of the message. If you were to place a numerical value on them it would be 95 style to 5 content. This doesn't mean that content is 90 points less important than style, it just emphasizes that without a high impact style the content gets drowned out in the apathy created by the lacklustre style of the communicator. Review the style of your delivery right now. Does it need upgrading?

Your clothes and hair communicate too

How do you dress? How often do you get your hair cut or styled? What colour suit do you wear? This is very important to get right if you want your delegates to take you seriously. Let me explain.

Both men and women must make sure that they wear a suit that is the right style and colour for them. If you don't then you will be telling the audience something about yourself that you may not want told. Don't undo all the hard work of preparation by undermining your credibility and personal image with ignoring something so easy to get right with a little bit of research and effort. Here are a few pointers that I've discovered over the years, which prove that networking with a variety of other professions, in this case an image consultant, can be useful.

Men with short legs should avoid trousers with turn-ups as they will make them appear even shorter and give the impression that they are not as tall as they aspire to be. While not a major issue to wrestle with in the scheme of things, is this what you really want to impress on people? A nickname from your delegates may be a term of endearment. However, inadvertently being referred to as 'the SMART stumpy one', as they discuss your sessions in the hotel bar after you have retired for the night, may not be quite what you had in mind when you planned to make an impact on your audience.

Double-breasted suits also have a similar effect on the shorter person and are best worn by taller people. They can also make a rounded figure look even more so. Single-breasted jackets are fine so long as they are not straining at the middle button.

For men, ties look best if they are colour co-ordinated with the suit and shirt and are knotted with the neat and symmetrical 'Windsor knot'; the bottom of the tie also needs to meet with the top of the belt buckle.

If you are overweight and don't want to admit it, at least be honest where your clothes are concerned. This applies much more to men than women. So many times I see a male trainer at the front of a group in a shirt that appears to be defying the laws of physics, with a tie that was last seen worn like that in public by Oliver Hardy. Come on guys, invest in a shirt that doesn't resemble a chef's giant icing bag bulging to overfill; you deserve better for yourself. True professionals care about their own appearance for the sake of others, as well as for themselves. I am not being 'fatist', just making the observation that clothes that fit, no matter the size, look better and feel a lot more comfortable. This little change will invariably improve the way you feel about yourself and you will no longer draw as much attention to yourself through ill-fitting clothes that emphasize your size unnecessarily.

Also, don't wear socks that are too short. I always opt for the extra-long sock, in the appropriate colour for the suit I'm wearing, obviously.

There is nothing worse than seeing a mass of hairy leg on show between the top of your sock and bottom of your trouser leg when you're sat down. It looks untidy and out of keeping with someone who purports to be a professional.

If you wear your hair short, make sure you get a trim at least once a month. This keeps everything tidy, and makes it easy to deal with getting ready on mornings when the hotel electricity supply is cut off at daybreak and throws all the electronic early morning calls out of sync. I've experienced this along with real fire alarms where panicking hotel staff made Basil Fawlty look the epitome of self-restraint, and a room with just a mattress laid on the floor. Not all at the same hotel I may add.

Do you prefer to wear red? A grey suit or navy blue skirt? Have you ever considered a brown suit? What style of suit or dress is best? The colour of our clothes has a large bearing on how we appear to others. This is because our natural colouring, ie hair, eyes and skin tone, will either complement the colour of the clothes we're wearing or clash horribly. You can check this out quite easily for yourself. Some colours when next to our skin will make us look pale and washed out, while others make us appear healthy and alert. This is one of those self-development areas: learn the basics about self-presentation and image, it will pay you back handsomely in the way people react to you and in your being able to influence them better.

On a different level, we know that red depicts aggression, or in its milder form strong authority. Grey and blue give the air of business-like authority, and brown in my opinion is best avoided like the plague unless you want to give the impression of a 1980s insurance salesman. I use the term 'salesman' consciously because I don't have a problem with women wearing brown. On women it's great, on men it just doesn't work in the training profession.

The way you dress is not to be treated flippantly. Remember it is impossible not to communicate and, as we discovered at the beginning of this chapter, before people get to know you they will take a good look. Then the judgements will be made. I know that it's a tired cliché but you really do only get one chance to make a first impression and never is that more true than in the training profession.

There are two great books on the market that really do work when it comes to creating the right image through our dress and I've included them in the reading list at the back of this book – *Presenting Yourself* (separate editions for both men and women).

So, make the right impression. It is your job, as a SMART trainer, to hook people into your delivery of the important topic of improved personal performance. Your company or your client is counting on you to make the difference when training their people new skills. They are looking to you to transfer the knowledge and the techniques that you possess so that their people can benefit themselves, their department and the company's bottom line. It is what we are all there to do, it is our key purpose. Fail to deliver this and we fail our profession and undermine its integrity.

Create the wrong opening message and you can set yourself up for a much tougher job in achieving the success you have worked so hard to accomplish. Do yourself, your profession and your delegates a favour: make sure you are informed enough to get those opening messages right first time.

A TRUE PROFESSIONAL IN EVERY SENSE

Everybody I have ever come across, and there have been many thousands over my years in the training profession, has always shown a strong interest in both behaving as a true professional and being treated like one. There are only two ways to guarantee that this will happen: 1) You will have to ensure that you communicate to others as a true professional; and 2) You will have to ensure that you look the part, in all areas of your appearance.

It is worth bearing in mind that the only reality is the perception of the people you are dealing with. How do they see and hear you? Does the overall message that you communicate when you deal with delegates, bosses or clients work in harmony with the 'professional' image you are endeavouring to create? Check it out objectively today and if necessary commit yourself to a personal upgrade. Do it now. Becoming a SMART trainer is not any one element; as you have explored and discovered here it is the whole 'professional' package delivered as seamlessly as possible.

We will now summarize this important chapter and move on to the completion of your Action Plan. Please scan the summary and prepare yourself with the relevant notes you have taken along the way, in particular the appropriate sections of both Chapters 4 and 8.

The SMART trainer's summary of Chapter 11

In summary, you covered, learnt and worked on the following key factors that will help you achieve Beyond Traditional Training status by investing in your own development and becoming a SMART trainer. You:

- discovered the critical piece of the SMART trainer's skills jigsaw;
- learnt how the jigsaw worked;
- learnt how to keep the jigsaw connected and flowing;
- discovered how crucial a role the central jigsaw piece played:
- discovered the power of the image you communicate;
- learnt the vital importance of generating credibility with your audience;
- learnt the key difference between style and content;
- discovered how your appearance communicates to your audience;
- learnt that the SMART trainer is the whole package.

Notes

1. No offence to gardeners intended here. All gardeners should be dressed appropriately for muck spreading. In the right setting this is perfectly acceptable and befitting the image of gardeners.
2. I won't say 100 per cent as I know that with people there are no absolutes and there is bound to be some sad person who prefers the comfort of a boring trainer.

12

THE SMART TRAINER METHODS FOR YOU TO ACTION – ACTION PLAN PART III

'Goals. There's no telling what you can do when you are inspired by them. There's no telling what you can do when you believe in them. And there's no telling what will happen when you act upon them.'

(Jim Rohn)

Your learning objectives in this chapter

By studying the inputs and activities in this chapter you will have:

- learnt how you build rapport and persuade people to want to learn;
- learnt how to run powerful delegate led workshops and training courses;
- further re-capped and consolidated the key learning points you have achieved so far in order to run fantastic training events;
- completed your step-by-step action plan for SMART trainer status;
- produced your blueprint plan of key actions to follow for achieving peak performance as a SMART trainer.

NOW SOME 'HOW TO' FOR YOUR KNOW-HOW

This is the final chapter of your programme. I will now guide you through a number of brief yet highly informative and instructive inputs that will give you a number of key activities that you will be able to run on your own courses and workshops immediately. First though, we'll explore the crucial skill of rapport-building in order to establish a sound relationship with your delegates.

Continual development of people skills

When a trainer's specialist subject is human psychology, assertiveness training, and interpersonal and communication skills, then his or her level of competence in this area is extremely high. After all, it's something they have studied for years, and are still studying. They have repeated all the key skills and strategies through running countless training courses in all of the main subject areas.

I have found that the trainers that have the hardest time with this area of people skills are those whose specialist areas are in technical disciplines, like engineers and technicians. They are brilliant on their specialist subject, and they probably know the core technicalities of training, but of course that in itself isn't enough. It is in the trainer/delegate relationship area that they so often fall down. They just don't have enough knowledge and practical experience at using the main communication strategies that help create the necessary rapport. And this is why they encounter a general air of indifference or neutrality within their training groups.

Difficult delegates

When this type of trainer is faced with potential conflict with a difficult delegate, they either ignore it or make the situation worse, or they react in a negative or aggressive way and make the situation unbearable.

These are the trainers that we now know as NIGHTMARE trainers. If you find yourself facing such scenarios every now and then, take a look at your skills in handling conflict and confrontation. Are you aware that you could be throwing fuel on to the proverbial fire by communicating with your audience or a particular person in the 'parent' ego state? This is a major cause of conflict within the workplace and relationships in general.

If you are not familiar with the term or process, you need to find out. All SMART trainers have a good understanding of transactional analysis, body language, motivational techniques, neurolinguistic programming, assertiveness techniques, questioning skills, active listening and positive phrasing. If you are missing any of these then you can begin working on them through your Action Plan. There are scores of books, audiotapes and workshops available on these crucial subject areas and you should find something to suit your preferred learning style.

Mastery in these skill areas will increase your performance in quantum leaps. Believe me, this is what happened to my career when I discovered this and then set about putting it into action in all areas of my life. You will become so tuned to people and the way they communicate that you will build rapport with people automatically through being able to communicate on the dual levels of conscious thought as well as the subconscious.

THE SMART TRAINER AND DIPLOMACY

Diplomacy and tact are the SMART trainer's motto; they are ambassadors of the profession and work hard at maintaining all of the relationships they are involved in. This is essential in order to ensure that they get the best from their delegates at all times during their programmes. Being a master of diplomacy requires that you become competent in the skill of rapport-building.

Making a real connection with your audience

How do you get people who have been sent on your training course to want to be there and actually learn something? The best technique I have found is to really be there and observe with all of your senses. By this I mean you put into practice the master skills of active listening so that you can communicate back to them a subtle reflection of the way they sound and the phrases they use. You need to observe and to reflect back their body language through the skill of mirroring and pacing. If you're unfamiliar with these tried and tested techniques that really do work, then make it your business to learn more about them. I can assure you it will pay you back handsomely.

With your focus being 'outward', your main concern will be your delegates and their wellbeing at all times. Remember, whatever you feel will be demonstrated through your body language. Ensure that your body language is always open; your arms should not be folded across your chest. And avoid pointing, with either finger or flipchart pen. Your eye contact should be consistent and evenly distributed throughout the group.

You must really pay attention to what they are saying, how they are saying it, the words they use and the body language they display. What I have described here are some of the key elements of rapport-building. Let's have a look at the main elements that go to establish this essential area of influential communication.

Research shows that one or a combination of the following elements affects the way we build rapport with people:

Age	Values
Goals	Accent
Interests	Education
Beliefs	Background
Faith	Class

If your audience detects that you are communicating to them in a patronizing or condescending way, you can rest assured that they will react back to you with rather negative behaviour. How exactly this will be displayed will depend on the level and mix of the group.

DELEGATE DRIVEN TRAINING COURSES

The simplest way of getting this right before you become a master in the art of rapport-building is to practise the 'outward focus' process we discussed earlier in this programme.

To help you do this you can build into your training courses a series of activities that help create the process of delegate driven training. You were briefly introduced to these earlier and in fact carried out one of them for your own personal development action plan.

I will now introduce you to delegate driven training courses and will take you through three of the easiest methods. There are many more, and you will discover these as you progress through your Action Plan. From my own personal experience of using them on a regular basis in my workshops and training programmes, they are the most effective for building great rapport and getting even the most negative of delegates to take an interest in the events ahead. They are:

1. The structured introduction interview.
2. The personal SWOT analysis.
3. Buzz groups.

While SMART trainers have prepared well for all of their training events, well in advance of them running, it is always the essential ingredient of delegate power that they know must never be left out. The SMART trainer has discovered the importance of getting people to take control of and therefore responsibility for their own learning.

While a structure will be in place and the overall objectives set, a belief among delegates that the course really is delegate driven will ensure a higher rate of participation and buy-in to the desired outcomes of the event. To achieve this the SMART trainer uses a number of simple yet very effective training tools as early into the course as possible. Where better to start than with the structured introduction interview?

The structured introduction interview

The purpose of this short session is to allow you, the trainer, some settling in time and to relax the delegates in order to prime them for the new information and skills that you want them to learn.

You pair up delegates in your group if even numbers allow, or use a mix of pairs and threes. You debrief the questions that you want the delegates to use to interview their partner. You can explain that you use this method because you have found that people prefer to talk about someone else rather than themselves at the opening of courses.

The questions can be a general mix of information-gathering such as the obvious name and location, job title, job responsibilities, etc. The critical question is: 'What do you want to gain from attending this workshop?' It is essential that you brief the delegates to give a detailed answer to this question. I tell the delegates that when they get to this question in their interview with their partner they are to ensure that they get them to be as specific as possible and I give them some examples related to the course I am running. If it is communication skills for instance, the answer may be, 'I want to be able to deal with conflict more successfully'.

I keep the list to about six or seven questions, with the last question something about themselves, like hobbies or interests, to prevent everything being focused on work. It is essential that your delegates are encouraged all the way through this little session to get comfortable and gain the information about their partner by asking the questions and listening and noting down the answers in their own words.

Having allowed the group about 10 minutes in total (15 if you have any groups of three, of course) get them in turn to introduce to you and the group the person they interviewed. By the end everyone will have had the opportunity to be vocal in front of the whole group, discussing the details of someone else. This is a great 'relaxer' for both delegates and trainer. It also allows you to observe their body language and speech patterns.

Having thanked them for their efforts in the introductions you then tell them that you will now build on that crucial question that they all found a little difficult to answer specifically – 'What do you want to gain from this programme?' You then lead them into the personal SWOT analysis.

The personal SWOT analysis

This is a fantastic session that always receives great reviews. It's something that most people either don't do very often or don't do at all, yet once they have done it they realize just how useful it is. This is how I run it on my programmes.

Following on from the introductions I cover the course objectives, the course methods that will be used in order to achieve those objectives, and the style of the course. Regarding the style of the course I use terms such as: informal, relaxed, open-minded, non-judgemental and so on, always ending with 'fun'. It is important to pause briefly on 'non-judgemental' and emphasize that no one will be judging anyone on the course. This is because everyone is here to learn and if there is to be any feedback then it will be positive and constructive. This is important because most people fear attending courses because they believe they will judged like they were at school. So I allay that fear as quickly as possible.

I then emphasize that this is their course and I want to ensure that they get exactly what they came here to achieve. I then tell them that in order for me to tailor the course to ensure that they achieve what they want, we will now complete a simple and quick exercise called the 'Personal SWOT analysis'. I check their understanding of the term SWOT and explain how it works.

I then get them to produce a set of four quadrants and to label them Strengths, Weaknesses, Opportunities and Threats. I then share with them the focus statement, which is tailored to the subject and objectives of the course, finishing off with a quick example for each quadrant in relation to the focus statement.

They then complete the exercise individually for about 10 minutes while I keep an eye on them and go to any who appear to be struggling in order to help them out. At the end of the 10 minutes I then set the rules for the review/feedback process. I explain that I will begin with the 'threats' quadrant and I will go to each person in turn and ask them to give me just one of the items in that quadrant. This is to ensure no one person lists half a dozen and demotivates those waiting to give input by saying all the items they had listed as well.

When each quadrant has one item from each delegate in it I then ask for any that have not been listed. I then give a brief input on how the course will work on this issue, explode that myth, develop that weakness, and build on that strength. I then point out that the items listed in the 'opportunities' quadrant are their motivators, their reasons for wanting to learn new skills on this course and to be able to practise them on their return to their workplace.

This session usually takes us up to the morning break and allows us to begin working on the key activities that I have programmed into the course immediately on our return.

As you can tell from the way both of these sessions (introductions and SWOT) are designed, the delegates start to see and therefore believe that this learning experience is, to a degree, within their control. This increases their interest levels and motivators to get involved. This purpose-built process acts as an extra lubricant to the rapport-building that begins the second you stand up in front of the group.

Now let's look at something that you can use a later on in the course.

How to use buzz groups

These little gems come into the course after it has been going for a few hours. What's a buzz group? Oh they're great. Once you've learnt how to form them and use them on your courses and workshops you'll wonder how you ever coped without them.

A buzz group is made up of two to four people who discuss a point or a problem for a short period of time, say between 2 and 15 minutes. Buzz groups are a great way to get the immediate reaction of the group to something. They are good for breaking up a theory session and can be used to raise the energy of the group if it begins to drop.

Break the group into pairs, threes or fours, depending on the size of your training course, then get them to take turns to discuss a particular point or issue that has been raised on the course. You might, for example, ask them to check their understanding of the learning points so far. You could also use it as a way of reviewing the previous day's learning. You could ask them to discuss the relevance of the last session or activity to what they do at work and how they might put it into practice. Another great use of buzz groups is to ask the delegates to identify any questions about the training sessions so far.

You can use buzz groups quite often but if you do, ensure you vary the questions and activities or they will become boring.

Remember buzz groups get their name from the noisy buzz they generate as people share their views and have their say, so be ready for a sudden increase in noise level when you set them going.

I have found them most useful after a theory session where the subject has been quite serious. A buzz group straight after this to discuss the key learning points and calls to action gets the energy levels back up and the delegates ready for a practice activity.

Buzz groups work well when the task or topic is easily understood or the discussion does not require too much thought. It's helpful to use a buzz group session when:

- You want everyone to have a chance to talk.
- You want to change focus from a previous session.
- You want to change the atmosphere.
- You have forgotten what you meant to do next and need to find your notes (use a topic like 'What have you learnt so far?').
- You want to wake everyone up.
- You want to get a lively discussion started and need to develop some opinions first.

Try using them the next time you run a course you are very familiar and comfortable with. Be warned though: once a buzz group session has been started it's not always easy to stop.

I encourage you to build these sessions into your own programmes and enjoy the difference they make to your training experience and of course the effectiveness of the delegates' learning.

THINKING INHIBITORS

We will now start work on your Action Plan. You will begin by identifying the thinking processes you use that hold back your self-development progress. These processes are called 'thinking inhibitors'.

The following thinking inhibitors will slow down your progress, so work at identifying them and then getting them out of your day-to-day thinking patterns. Remember we are all creatures of habit so the way you think can be changed. Use the four-step process and the 21-day rule and get rid of those thinking inhibitors for good.

Check down the list and circle the inhibitors that you recognize in your own behaviours and attitudes. Then build the relevant change actions into your Action Plan in order to remove them from your life.

Self-doubt	Intimidation	Lack of interest	Impatience
Interruption	Perfectionism	Cynicism	Anxiety
Ridicule	Stereotyping	Distraction	Jealousy
Shame	Low expectations	Competition	Hierarchy
Rigid adherence to policy		Absence of appreciation	

WHAT IS IT YOU REALLY WANT?

Spend at least 15 minutes answering the following questions. All of them will enable you to clarify the exact content of your Action Plan so that you can achieve the consistent behaviours of the SMART trainer.

Please answer with total honesty. Once you have answered each of the questions you can proceed on to the re-drafting of your key actions.

YOUR SMART TRAINER ACTION PLAN QUESTIONS

What specifically do you want with regard to becoming a SMART trainer?

When, where, with whom do you want it?

What do you need in order to accomplish this?

How will you know when you have it?

What will you see, hear and feel?

What will you look like, sound like?

What will happen if you get this result?

What won't happen if you get it?

What won't happen if you don't get it?

How do you know it's worth getting?

How will achieving this affect your life? Your family? Your business or job?

What will be different as a result of having this?

What will it be like when you have this?

THE THREE STEPS TO SELF-BELIEF

To build on the answers you have just given you have to put into action a plan that is designed to enhance your self-belief. The key attributes that all SMART trainers have are a strong self-belief and a positive attitude. Another of their philosophies is the 'You can' philosophy. This goes:

> You can if you think you can.
> If you think you can't you're right!

They are people who operate with a totally positive mental attitude, also known as PMA.

PMA is a prerequisite for success. Potential is not developed through a negative attitude. You choose! So choose the route to great fortune. SMART trainers are so successful because they have PMA and operate to the 'P' thought process, which goes:

> Positive people provide!
> Positive people persist!
> Positive people perform!
> Positive people have personal power!
> Positive people get noticed!

A major element of your achieving the success as a trainer that you deserve and so strongly desire is your self-belief in doing so. Self-belief is the catalyst to the actions you take, which, as we know from the universal law of cause and effect, will determine the outcome you receive. Will it be the outcome you desire, in this case becoming a SMART trainer, or will it be something that falls well short? The power to achieve or under-achieve is in your control.

Take a moment to work on these three simple steps to self-belief. Once you have the information logged then you can build this into your Action Plan.

The three steps

Step 1: True success is... (write down exactly what it is to you)

Step 2: My personal blockages to success are... (write down anything that you feel stops you achieving)

Step 3: My fears about success are... (what is it about success that you believe will spoil your life as it is now?)

With these boxes completed you will now be able to recognize exactly where you have to adjust your self-belief and develop your attitudes and skills in order to establish a sound self-belief system that will deliver you to your desired outcome. In the appendix you will find a list of SMART trainer affirmations, which you can use to practise saying over and over. This is a great self-belief building exercise, which I strongly recommend you use as often as you can.

TIME TO REVISIT YOUR FINDINGS FOR YOUR ACTION PLAN

You can now update the information in each of the areas within this framework. Re-list all the appropriate information, which you have collected through the previous input session in this section, and add it to or adjust the information you collected in the previous sections (Chapters 4 and 8).

Go through framework one and two now and update any areas that you feel are relevant in light of what you have covered in Part Three of your programme. List the information in Tables 12.1 and 12.2.

Table 12.1 *Framework 1*

Skill levels, attitudes and behaviours I have identified as being an obstacle to achieving my goal of SMART trainer	*Key recommendations required to initiate improvement in my performance and effectiveness as a trainer*

YOUR ACTION PLAN – FINAL DRAFT

Using the information you have gathered on your current performance behaviours you can now complete the following Blueprint Action Plan. You will see that it is in two parts. The first section gets you to answer the five questions of performance. Once this section is completed you will then commit yourself to the key actions that will ensure you will achieve your desired outcome.

Table 12.2 *Framework 2*

Current Assets

Strengths	*Key skills used*

Identified Potential

Hidden strengths to develop	*New skills/knowledge required*

Key Changes That Need to Occur

Attitude/behaviours displayed	*Changes recommended*

Section 1: the five questions of performance

My goal is to become a SMART trainer operating to the SMART trainer code of conduct and performing consistently to the SMART trainer behaviours.

Now answer the following five questions:

1. How would I like my performance to be?
2. Why would I like it to be like that?

3. What is my performance like now?
4. What could I do to improve?
5. When will I start?

You can complete the action planner in Table 12.3, which you can later transfer to your daily 'to do' list and personal development scheduler, which you should hold in your time management system.

Table 12.3 *The key actions I intend to carry out immediately*

1.	2.
3.	4.
5.	6.
7.	8.
9.	10.
11.	12.

YOU ARE NOT ALONE

This is nothing to do with UFO theories or the 'X Files' but has everything to do with a support programme that you may wish to take advantage of. During your journey through this programme you will have discovered many things about yourself. Some of these will be strengths and some weaknesses.

My personal philosophy as you will recall is, 'Your success is my success' and to prove that I really do believe that and live by it I want to offer you my help and guidance as a coach. Please feel free to contact me via e-mail in the first instance with your query or question that you would like an answer to. I promise that I will reply as quickly as I am able. I feel that this is important, especially when working through my Master Class programme in this book. After all, if you had attended the three-day workshop programme then you would have had opportunities to speak to me direct and ask questions as they arose. So once again my e-mail address is: kencoach@aol.com

REVERSING YOUR WAY TO IMPROVEMENT

At the back of this book is a list of books and audiotapes that I have come across in my years as a trainer and consultant. I have all of the books that are listed there in my own business library so that I can dip in and out of them at will as I research articles, books and of course training and development programmes that I am commissioned to design.

One of the most well-thumbed books is a great volume, *Workshops that Work*, by Tom Bourner, Vivien Martin and Phil Rice. It contains 100 ideas that make your training events more effective. I would like to share with you number 13 (I hope you're not superstitious), which is headed 'How to run a disastrous workshop'. I believe that it is a great piece to end our programme on. I hope that once you've read it you will see why. Here's what it says.

HOW TO RUN A DISASTROUS WORKSHOP

If you know how to make something worse, then you know how to make it better. A useful technique for problem solving is to look for ways to make a situation as bad as it can be, then to examine all these ways to looking for how to reverse them. This should lead you to a recipe for brilliant success.

- Don't plan anything.
- Don't book a venue.
- Don't advertise (or publicise) the workshop.
- Don't tell anyone about it.
- Tell everyone the wrong time and venue.
- Book an unsuitable venue:
  - too small;
  - too large;
  - too dark;
  - stuffy;
  - smelly;
  - noisy;
  - bad acoustics;
  - cold/hot;
  - no drinks;

  - no food;
  - unfriendly;
  - no chairs/tables;
  - no equipment.
- Don't have any coffee breaks – or any breaks.
- Make sure that the only available refreshment is coffee.
- Don't introduce yourself.
- Don't give the participants the opportunity to introduce themselves.
- Talk all the time.
- Don't let anyone else talk or do anything.
- Don't tell anyone what the programme is.
- Don't have a programme.
- Don't tell anyone your aims.
- Start late.
- Go to lunch late.
- Finish late.
- Don't tell anyone you are the facilitator.
- Tell everyone that it is much too hard for them to do.
- Keep repeating the same activity.
- Don't bother to debrief any of the activities.
- Don't make eye contact with anyone.
- Don't send out a map.
- Set 15-minute coffee breaks when the coffee is being served in another building.
- Don't include the option of a vegetarian lunch.
- Say 'I am the world's expert on…'.

I'm sure that you could add to this list. Make a point of carrying out this exercise as part of your own self-improvement programme on a regular basis in order to stay alert to the quality of your courses and programmes.

Take a look at each of these points in turn and reverse them; this will then become your checklist for running a good workshop. Plan everything, book a venue, advertise the workshop, etc. Save your checklist and add to it each time that you plan a workshop.

ONE LAST COMMENT

I will leave you now to get on with the exciting task of becoming a SMART trainer and I look forward to the day when our paths will cross, as all SMART trainers' paths surely do as we journey through this life of adventures and achievements. I will just share with you one last piece of wisdom that I came across many years ago now and still use to close some of my workshops:

> There are three types of people in this world,
> There are those that make things happen,
> Those that watch things happen,
> And those who look bewildered and say,
> Er, what happened?

Just make sure you belong to the first group. Well done and every success.

The SMART trainer's summary of Chapter 12

In summary, you covered, learnt and worked on the following key factors that will help you achieve Beyond Traditional Training status by investing in your own development and becoming a SMART trainer:

- you learnt about the SMART trainer and the art of building rapport;
- you learnt how to focus your courses to become delegate driven;
- you discovered how to use the 'structured interview' and the personal SWOT analysis;
- you learnt how and when to use buzz groups;
- you discovered your thinking inhibitors;
- you decided what it is that you really want;
- you completed your Action Plan questions;
- you learnt how to use the three steps of self-belief;
- you completed the final draft of your Action Plan;
- you discovered that you are not alone;
- you decided which group of people you wanted to belong to.

SMART TRAINER AFFIRMATIONS

The following affirmations should be repeated as often as you are able. Get yourself into the SMART Trainer habit of self-disciplined positive affirmations. Repeat any, or the entire list:

- I am strong and decisive.
- I know I am successful, confident and respected.
- I am creative and imaginative.
- I am inspirational and I can bring joy.
- My delegates enjoy being trained by me.
- I am relaxed and happy.
- I always manage to make customers feel relaxed.
- Delegates can trust me and have confidence in me.
- I am loving and also loved by others.

You do not have to stick with just this list; make your own list of positive affirmations written in the same style.

RECOMMENDED READING AND AUDIOTAPES

Here is a selection of books that I have found to be of particular use when working on my own self-development Action Plan. I have also listed a number of audiotape sets, which are great for filling that dead time while travelling on business. All of the books listed below are an important part of my own business library that I have created since I began working as a training professional. I use them as reference guides and sources of inspiration on a regular basis as part of my work.

THE BOOKS

Bandler, R and Grinder, J (1990) *Frogs into Princes*, Eden Grove Editions, Enfield

Bentley, T (1991) *The Business of Training*, McGraw-Hill, Maidenhead

Berne, E (1964) *Games People Play*, Penguin, Harmondsworth

Bourner, T, Martin, V and Rice, P (1993) *Workshops that Work*, McGraw-Hill, Maidenhead

Chopra, D (1994) *The Seven Spiritual Laws of Success*, Amber-Allen, San Rafael, CA

Covey, S R (1992) *The Seven Habits of Highly Effective People*, Simon & Schuster, London

Crainer, S (1998) *The Ultimate Business Library*, Capstone, Oxford

Decker, B (1992) *You've Got to be Believed to be Heard*, William Morrow, New York

Foster, T R V (1991) *101 Ways to Generate Great Ideas*, Kogan Page, London
Hill, N (1966) *Think and Grow Rich*, Melvin Powers Wiltshire, Hollywood
Jeffers, S (1991) *Feel the Fear and Do It Anyway*, Random House, London
Lancaster, G (1993) *The 20% Factor*, Kogan Page, London
Lehmkuhl, D (1995) *Organizing for the Creative Person*, Kogan Page, London
Pease, A (1988) *Body Language*, Sheldon Press, London
Pease, A and Garner, A (1989) *Talk Language*, Simon & Schuster, London
Pipe, S (1993) *101 Ways to Run your Business Profitably*, Kogan Page, London
Race, P and Smith, B (1995) *500 Tips for Trainers*, Kogan Page, London
Robbins, A (1991) *Awaken the Giant Within*, Simon & Schuster, New York
Rohn, J (1996) *The Treasury of Quotes*, Health Communications, Florida
Smith, H W (1994) *The 10 Natural Laws of Successful Time & Life Management*, Nicholas Brealey, London
Spillane, M (1993) *Presenting Yourself – A personal image guide for men*, Piatkus, London
Spillane, M (1993) *Presenting Yourself – A personal image guide for women*, Piatkus, London
Stewart, I and Joines, V (1987) *TA Today*, Lifespace, Kegworth

THE AUDIOTAPES

Brooks, M, *Instant Rapport*, Simon & Schuster Audio, London
Covey, S R, *The Seven Habits of Highly Effective People*, Nightingale-Conant, Devon
Hill, N, *The Science of Personal Achievement*, Simon & Schuster Audio, London
McKenna, P and Breen, M, *The Power to Influence*, Nightingale-Conant, Devon
Rohn, J, *The Art of Exceptional Living*, Nightingale-Conant, Devon
Tracy, B, *Maximum Achievement*, Simon & Schuster Audio, London
Tracy, B and Rose, C, *Accelerated Learning Techniques*, Nightingale-Conant, Devon

Ziglar, Z, *Goals*, Simon & Schuster Audio, London

Everyone who is serious about becoming a success should have a personal library, and every library begins with just one book.

You can contact me at:

17 Beresford Drive
Sudbrooke
Lincoln
LN2 2YH
Tel: 01522 595947
Fax: 01522 752175
e-mail: kencoach@aol.com

INDEX